The Young Investor

Projects and Activities for Making Your Money Grow

Second Edition

Katherine R. Bateman

CHICAGO
REVIEW
PRESS

Library of Congress Cataloging-in-Publication Data

Bateman, Katherine Roberta.
  The young investor : projects and activities for making your money grow / Katherine
R. Bateman. — 2nd ed.
     p. cm.
  Includes index.
  ISBN 978-1-56976-546-3 (pbk.)
  1. Investments—Juvenile literature. 2. Saving and investment—Juvenile literature.
3. Money—Juvenile literature. 4. Stocks—Juvenile literature. 5. Children—
Finance, Personal—Juvenile literature. I. Title.

  HG4521.B4225 2010
  332.6—dc22

                                                                        2010025642

Cover design: Paul Dolan Illustration
Interior design and illustration: Sean O'Neill

Published by Chicago Review Press, Incorporated
814 North Franklin Street
Chicago, Illinois 60610
ISBN 978-1-56976-546-3
Printed in the United States of America
5 4 3 2 1

To my grandchildren—Eleanor, Arlo, T, Cauley,
Asa, Summer, and Roger Clay

Contents

3

All About Investing

4

All About the Market

5

All About Stock Tables

6

All About the Economy

7

All About Stock Picking

8

All About All of the Above

Conclusion

ACKNOWLEDGMENTS

The following people deserve warm thanks:

Sara Schastok, for serving as matchmaker between my book and Chicago Review Press.

The staff of Chicago Review Press, who graciously walked me through each step of publishing a first book, then another book, and now this revision.

Cary Anderson, who provided me with first-hand information on credit unions.

T, who searched for interesting number stories and found them.

Billy Ray Fawns, for being so open and forthcoming about each step of his saving and investment plans. His story carries the concepts of investing into reality.

Finally, Richard, who has helped me build a contented, creative base from which to work.

A Letter to Parents and Grandparents

OR WHY I WROTE THIS BOOK

In 1996, WHEN my oldest grandchild turned 10—or "moved into double digits," as she said—I made plans to give money to each of my grandchildren when they reached their teenage years. I wanted to teach them a respect for money and how to invest it, but most of all I wanted them to be comfortable with money and investing concepts. I wanted them to know what people were talking about when they discussed emerging markets, rising interest rates, or consumer spending. I wanted them to be fluent in the language of business.

That summer I began to jot down notes to include in a short set of guidelines. My notes expanded over time as I realized that there was more to tell than the actual investment process. I needed to teach them about savings, but I also needed to discuss the concept of money. I wanted my grandchildren to understand some basic things about the economy, to become familiar with terms like *inflation* and *recession* and government agencies such as the Board of Governors of the Federal Reserve. I wanted them to know how and why major weather events affect investments. I wanted them to know how to read the stock tables in the *Wall Street Journal* or the *New York Times* or online.

My notes continued to grow. By this time I also had a set of cards with definitions. I've always appreciated glossaries, so I decided I would give my grandkids one too, as well as phone numbers and Web addresses so they could have additional resources at their fingertips. When it was all done, I had a lengthy set of guidelines and a huge pile of scratch-paper notes that totaled a book's worth of material. In the process of thinking through and collecting this material, I talked to my friends about what I was doing for my grandchildren. Their response was always the same: "When you get the book done, will you give me copies for my kids and one for me? I need to learn about it, too." That's how this book was created.

I have written for children of that in-between—or "tween"—age. That's the tone. The data is ageless. *The Young Investor* provides guidance on various types of savings plans and explains the difference between compound and simple interest. I describe Wall Street, the Dow Jones Industrial Average, and the economy. I teach young investors how to read stock and mutual fund tables.

This book also includes activities that provide hands-on experience with money and ways to make it grow. As the book continues, the concepts and activities become more complex, but readers will already have the tools to understand these from earlier chapters. My goal is to make individuals— whether they are 9, 12, or 40—conversant in saving and investing money.

This process is meant to be fun, educational, and—potentially— financially successful. When I first wrote the book, interest rates were high. Now, following the recession of 2008–2009, they are more modest. Yet compound interest still works miracles, and I urge everyone to start saving early. Just imagine what your kids and grandkids can do in the future if they have no fear of investing as teenagers and young adults.

—Katherine R. Bateman
January 2010

Introduction

THE WARM-UP, INCLUDING THE GOAL

STARTING WHEN I was little—six or seven—my mother and father made me put most of my birthday and Christmas money into a piggy bank to save for a bicycle. They had me do this even though, right then, I really wanted things like a candy bar or a comic book. Now I see they had the right idea, but it was only half right. If I had put my money into a real bank instead of my piggy bank, I would have accumulated the money for my bike much faster, because a bank would pay me to save my money. My money would have made more money.

The Young Investor is all about how to make your money make money. First I'll explain about money itself—what it is and how we buy it. I want to make you comfortable with the idea of saving and investing, and this book will give you the tools to do it.

The first time that many of you bought money was when you were born. Your grandparents may have paid you to struggle into this world by giving you a gift of money at your birth. Never mind that it was your mother who did most of the struggling—you were the one who received the money in some sort of savings account.

Next I'll cover the different ways to save money. Banks are not the only place to put your savings. You can also save your money at a special kind of company called a *credit union*, or you can buy something called a *certificate of deposit*. You can shop for the best deal on your savings money just as you do for a new pair of gym shoes endorsed by your favorite basketball star. Plus you'll learn about how your money can make more money by the power of compounding.

I'll then explore the investment world. Savers can also be investors. The question is what to invest in—stocks, bonds, or mutual funds or some of each. I'll explain each of these savings tools and what they do for you and your money. How to decide where to invest is a major focus of *The Young Investor*. I'll also explain how investment markets work.

I'll cover Wall Street next, including how it got its name and what people mean when they refer to "the market." This interesting story will give you clues about this country's history. You'll also learn about the different types of markets available for stock investments and how each one works.

Once you know about investments and how the market works, I'll teach you how to learn about particular stocks. In order to make good decisions, you'll need to know how to read certain stock tables in newspapers or online. Eventually you'll be able to show your friends how to do it.

Next I'll cover the economy and explain why floods and hurricanes affect you just as much as summers that are too hot or winters that are too cold. You may end up reading the paper, looking at the Weather Channel, and listening to world news. Knowing what's going on in the world may determine how much money you make on your investments, which in turn will affect how much you invest.

Next comes the reward—you'll select a stock for investment. There are hundreds of companies you can invest in by buying stock in those companies. Here I'll offer you some guidelines to help you narrow your stock choices. I'll show you how to figure out if the companies you think you want to invest in are good choices.

The final chapter provides a lot of information about making investments, including phone numbers, online resources, and books to read. You have to be a certain age to buy or sell stocks. If you're not that age, you'll have to tell an adult how to do it for you. When you reach 18 or 21 (depending on which state you live in), you'll be able to make these decisions and do these transactions yourself.

This book includes a glossary of terms for reference as you go through these chapters. It will also prove a handy resource for grown-ups to help them understand what you mean when you say something like, "Since the Fed seems to have shortened the recession with its easy-money policy, I think it's now safe to invest in one of the car companies."

To help you learn how to save and invest, I'm going to give you a real life example of someone who did—Billy Ray Fawns. I met Billy Ray in Mount Sterling, Kentucky, where I had a house. He mowed my lawn for me. One day, when we talked about his mowing business, I realized Billy Ray was born with a desire to save money. I won't tell you the whole story now. I'll just say that at age 6, Billy Ray made his first money, and by age 21, he had saved enough money to buy a piece of farmland. One more thing you should know about Billy Ray is that he was a basketball star in high school and college. People in Mount Sterling still know him as "the Legend."

I have friends in their 40s and 50s who are afraid to buy stock or mutual funds. They don't know how to begin choosing a stock or researching mutual funds or what to say when they make their choice. Even worse, they are embarrassed to ask questions for fear people will think they're dumb. I don't want that to happen to you. I want you to feel confident about saving and investing, about understanding the economy, and about picking stocks. I don't care whether you buy stocks or mutual funds; I just don't want you to be shy when it comes to asking questions about money. As you'll see, Billy Ray asked a lot of questions, and people loved to answer him. It made them feel good.

It's a good idea to be familiar with ideas and words that have to do with money. If you are, then when you get your first job you'll already know how to save, you'll understand the power of compounding (you'll learn about this in chapter 2), and you won't lose any time in saving for a car, a house, or some other expensive item.

Did you know that if you, with the help of your parents or grandparents, save $8,000 each year between the ages of 7 and 21 and place the money in a savings account that has an average interest rate of 4.5%, you will have $1,000,000 (actually $1,153,286) when you are 65? If you don't start saving until age 22, you will have to save $8,000 a year *every year* until age 65 to have your million. Just think about that!

Or how about this: Wait to get your first car until after college. Save $10,000 from gifts and part-time jobs by age 16. Then, instead of paying the expenses of driving a car in high school and college—which costs about $3,000 a year ($1,000 in gas to drive 8,000 miles at an average of 25 miles per gallon; $1,500 for car insurance; $500 for maintenance and repairs)—add that $3,000 to your savings until you are 21. Then forget about it. At an average interest rate of 4.5%, that $25,000 that you saved for five years will be worth $200,000 when you are 65. That's the power of compounding!

All About Money

WHAT IS IT, AND WHERE DOES IT COME FROM?

How to Buy Money

BEFORE YOU CAN save money, you need to have some to save. In the introduction I said you buy money. You can buy it in a number of ways. The most common way to buy money is in exchange for a skill you have. You can earn money for chores in your home, such as helping with dinner, taking out the trash, washing the family car, or doing yard work. You can earn it by babysitting in the neighborhood, by walking dogs for a dog-walking service, or by feeding and playing with your best friend's cat while her family is out of town.

Whatever the skill, the end result is that someone pays you for your effort. The amount you are paid depends on the level of skill or the length

1

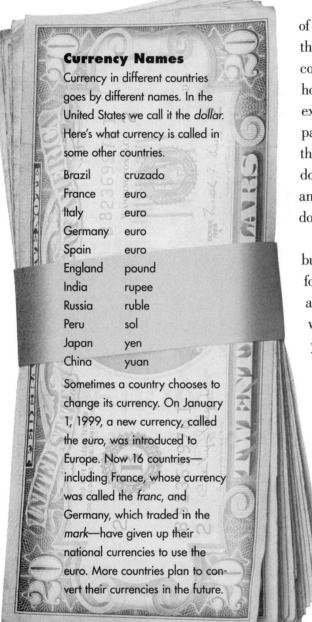

Currency Names

Currency in different countries goes by different names. In the United States we call it the *dollar*. Here's what currency is called in some other countries.

Brazil	cruzado
France	euro
Italy	euro
Germany	euro
Spain	euro
England	pound
India	rupee
Russia	ruble
Peru	sol
Japan	yen
China	yuan

Sometimes a country chooses to change its currency. On January 1, 1999, a new currency, called the *euro*, was introduced to Europe. Now 16 countries—including France, whose currency was called the *franc*, and Germany, which traded in the *mark*—have given up their national currencies to use the euro. More countries plan to convert their currencies in the future.

of time required to complete the job, and sometimes it's a combination of both. This is how people earn money: they exchange their skills for their paychecks. Then they take their paychecks and pay the dog groomer and the grocer and all the other people who do things for them.

Another common way to buy money is to exchange it for something you own, such as a sweater that you don't wear anymore, DVDs that you don't watch anymore, or vintage Star Wars figures that you received as a gift when you were 7. The amount you are paid is based on what you and the buyer think is a fair price. If either of you think the price is not fair, the exchange won't happen.

The History of Money

You've heard people—usually people like parents—say that money doesn't grow on trees. It doesn't. It doesn't actually grow anywhere. It's printed by the U.S. government or the Japanese government or the French or Nigerian governments. Every government prints its own money, or *currency*.

The first money was not metal coins or paper as we have now; the first money was salt. In ancient China, people paid for something they wanted to buy in salt. In ancient Rome, soldiers were paid in salt. The word for *salt* in Latin—the language the Romans used—was *sal*. When your parents talk about their *salaries*, they are using a word from the history of money, because *salaries* comes from *sal*.

Other things were also used to pay for the goods and services people needed. In some places, such as the Yap Islands, money was made from stone. In Fiji, whale teeth were used for money. In Africa, elephant hair was the currency. On the Solomon Islands, tobacco was used as money.

Around 2500 B.C.E., or about 4,500 years ago, precious metals like gold, silver, and copper began to be used as money. Coins found in the region of ancient Mesopotamia (now occupied by Iraq and parts of Syria, Turkey, and Iran) weren't perfect circles like our coins, but they did have pictures stamped on them as ours do today. You can find some of these coins at museums or coin collection shops.

Search for Old Coins

Go on a search for old coins. See if you can find a coin collector in your town. Search online for "coin collectors," or look in the phone book under "Coins." (If you can't find a listing under "Coins," look under "Numismatics," which means the study or collection of coins and paper money.) When you find a coin collector, ask an adult to take you to his or her store. When you arrive, ask the store owner to show you his or her oldest coins. Then ask the owner to tell you about those coins. If you say you're interested in numismatics, he or she will probably tell you a whole lot.

The Smithsonian Museum and the United States Treasury, both in Washington, D.C., have excellent coin collections, as do lots of museums around the country. If you can't go there in person, check out their sites online. For the Smithsonian, go to http://americanhistory.si.edu/

collections/index.cfm, then click on "Coins, Currency and Medals" under "Collection Subjects." The site for the U.S. Department of the Treasury is www.ustreas.gov/kids/. You can also go to your local library or school library and look for books on coins, or you can check the encyclopedia under "Coins" or "Numismatics." Your librarian can also help you search for pictures of coins online.

Paper money came much later than metal coins. The earliest surviving paper money is from China. It was issued a little before 1400 C.E. and was about the size of a piece of notebook paper. About 100 years before that, the Mongol warlord Kublai Khan used pieces of bark from mulberry trees for money.

Making Money in America

The United States Bureau of Engraving and Printing prints our paper money in two cities—Washington, D.C., and Fort Worth, Texas. Since money is worth a lot, there are many secrets regarding the making of money. One of the secrets is about the paper itself. We know that it's made from a mixture of linen and cotton. We also know that the paper has tiny colored nylon threads in it. But only a few people know the exact formula for making the paper on which our money is printed. Those people work for a company that has produced the paper for more than 100 years. Another secret is how the ink that is used to print on the money is made. It is slightly magnetic, but the formula is a carefully guarded secret.

To make money as fast as possible, multiple images of dollar bills are printed on large sheets of paper. After 100 sheets are printed, the money is cut into single bills. The stacks of bills are bundled together until they are approximately the size of a brick. These "money bricks" are then sent to banks, where people usually go to find crisp new bills.

Paper money in the United States comes in different amounts, called *denominations*. The denominations are $1, $5, $10, $20, $50, and $100.

The Bureau of Engraving and Printing used to print $500 and $1,000 bills, but these big denominations were primarily for banks. Individuals liked to order $500 and $1,000 bills for special occasions like a big birthday or retirement party, but now you can only find them in numismatic collections.

Our metal coins are made by the United States Mint in plants in Denver, San Francisco, and Philadelphia. The process of making coins is called *minting*. Each coin has a letter on it for the city where it was minted: *D* for Denver, *S* for San Francisco, and *P* for Philadelphia. (There are, however, a couple of exceptions. For example, Philadelphia was the first mint in the United States. Because there was only one place to mint coins then, there was no need to include a mint mark to tell where the coin was made. Lots of Lincoln pennies have no mint mark. Also, between 1965 and 1967, the Coinage Act of 1965 banned mint marks altogether.) Check your coins and see if you can find out where they were made. Special commemorative coins in gold and silver are minted in West Point, New York, where some of our gold and silver is stored. The bulk of our gold, however, is kept under lock and key in a huge fortified vault at the bullion depository in Fort Knox, Kentucky.

When metal was first used for money, the coins were made of precious metals like gold, silver, or copper. Now our coins are made from a mixture of copper and nickel, because there's more copper and nickel available than gold and silver. When someone talks about "the gold standard" or "the pound sterling," he or she is referring to a time when money was made from gold and silver. If you are interested in learning more about the history of money and how it is made today, the U.S. Department of the Treasury has a Web site that is fun to poke around on. Just go to www.ustreas. gov/education. You can even get a virtual tour of the Treasury and the various sites where coins are minted.

What happens if a bill gets so old it falls apart? If you have at least 51% of it, or just over half, it still counts as money and can be exchanged for a full bill at a bank. If the bank won't replace your torn bill, you can send it with a note of explanation to the U.S. Department of the Treasury, and they will usually send you a better one. But if you have only 49% of the bill, then you're out of luck. What you have is just a yucky, torn piece of scrap paper.

The Money Circle

Once money is printed, it's put into circulation. Circulation is a good word for it because money circles around and around, going from one person's hands to another's, over and over again. Sometimes this happens slowly and sometimes very quickly. Around holidays like Christmas, Hanukkah, and Kwanzaa, it can circle like a whirlwind!

Here's an example of how money circles. Your sister babysits for a little girl on the next block. She takes the money that she receives and buys a cashmere sweater that she's had her eye on for some time. The store where she buys the sweater pays the clerk who sold it to your sister for the time he worked. The clerk takes his salary and buys a white puppy with a black spot over its left eye. The dog breeder who sold the dog to the clerk takes the money the clerk gave him in exchange for the puppy and buys a calico kitten for his wife, who doesn't like dogs at all.

With all that circulation, paper money gets old and ratty and coins get so worn out that you can't read the mint mark. One-dollar bills last the shortest period of time—about 15 months—because they get circulated the most. Bills worth $5, $10, and $20 last longer since they don't change hands as often.

When money gets worn out, it must be replaced. So, when a really old bill or a really beat-up coin comes into a bank, the bank teller sets it aside to exchange for new money. Armored trucks take the old money from the banks to the Department of the Treasury. These bills are shredded into tiny strips, then the strips are burned until they turn into fluffs of white ash. The coins are sent to one of the three mints, dumped into a huge pot, and melted. The melted metal is then minted into new coins.

$ Make a Money Circle

Be a money detective and track a money circle. Starting with your allowance or the money you're paid for chores, write down where your money came from and where your money went. Go as far back as you can and as far forward as you can. See how close it comes to making a circle. Refer to the example on page 7 if you get stuck.

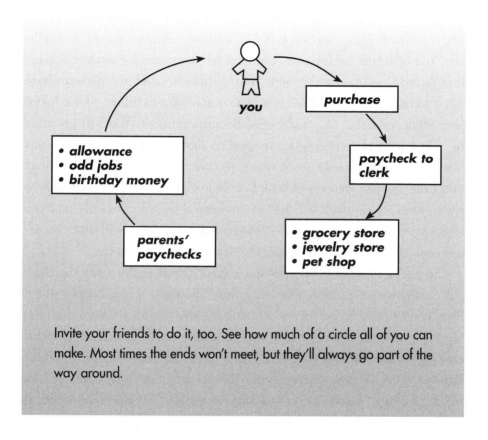

Invite your friends to do it, too. See how much of a circle all of you can make. Most times the ends won't meet, but they'll always go part of the way around.

Not All Money Is Printed with Secret Ink

Did you know that no cash actually changes hands for the majority of purchases in this country? About 60 years ago almost everything bought and sold was paid for with cash. Now we use other forms of money: Credit cards are often used when a person wants to pay for something and doesn't want to use cash. Checks are another common way to pay for things.

Many people keep money in banks. In order to keep track of everyone's money, the bank gives each person a number that applies only to that person's money. Your number is your *account number.* It's sort of like having a combination lock on your locker at school. All your stuff is safe from friends who want to borrow things without asking when it's locked in your own locker. There are many kinds of bank accounts. Right now, though, I'll talk just about checking accounts.

Here's how a checking account works: You have some birthday money and some cash from chores you did for a family member, friend, or neighbor. You take this money to a bank and tell someone at customer service that you want to open an account. You will be directed to a person whose job is to help you do just that. She gives you a form to fill out that asks for your name, address, age, and Social Security number. You will probably be asked for your mother's maiden name (her last name when she was born) or the name of the town where you were born. This is for security purposes, in case your checkbook is ever lost or stolen. Then you have to sign a form so the bank will be able to keep a record of exactly how you sign your name. If you are under 18 years old, the bank will make someone over 18 sign his or her name, too. It's the law.

So you've filled out the form and signed it, and you've given the bank the money you've earned. The bank then gives you a checkbook, which usually contains 25 checks and a check register (where you record all the checks you write to keep track of your money). A checkbook is small enough to carry around with you. When you carry your checks, you don't have to carry money. Many people like paying for things with checks exactly for this reason. If you lose your checkbook, it can be replaced. If you lose your cash, it's gone for good.

One cold winter afternoon you decide that you absolutely have to buy a new video game that your friends are talking about. So, instead of taking cash, you grab your checkbook and head to the nearest store that sells games. At the checkout counter you see a notice that says the store will accept checks if you have a picture ID. Since you have your school ID, you write out a check for $43.50. All you have to do is write in the date and the name of the store where it says "Pay to the order of." Then you write in the amount of the purchase—in this case, $43.50—in the box and then write out the amount in words on the line below that. (This can stump you sometimes—occasionally I forget how to spell "forty.") Next comes the easy part—signing your name—and then it's done. Hand it to the clerk and collect your game.

Even though your check is as good as cash, the store is not paid in cash by the bank. In fact, no cash actually changes hands. Instead, the bank takes money out of your account and puts it into the store's account. In other words, the bank transfers funds from one account to another, and it does it all electronically. But there's a catch: the bank will only transfer funds if you have funds to transfer. Your balance, or the total amount of money you have in your account, must be larger than your check amount. The check register in your checkbook is designed to help you keep track of your money. Your check register is where you record an entry every time you write a check. Your register will look like the one below. Each time you write a check, you fill in the number from the top right-hand corner of the check, the date the check was written, the name of the store or person you wrote the check to, and the amount. Then you subtract this amount from your balance. That way you can keep track of just how much money you have in your account at all times.

NUMBER	DATE	DESCRIPTION OF TRANSACTION	PAYMENT DEBIT (-)	√	FEE (IF ANY) (-)	DEPOSIT CREDIT (+)	BALANCE
		RECORD ALL CHARGES OR CREDITS THAT AFFECT YOUR ACCOUNT					$1000 00
116	3/11	Sports Plus	61 50				938 50
117	3/20	Barbara's Books	36 17				902 33
	3/15	deposit - b'day check				50 00	952 33
118	4/2	School Colors	89 00				863 33

REMEMBER TO RECORD AUTOMATIC PAYMENTS/DEPOSITS ON DATE AUTHORIZED

The bank will also help you keep track of the checks you've written. Once a month the bank sends you something called a *statement*. A statement lists every check you've written over the past month, all the deposits you've made, and any fees they've charged you. A *deposit* is the banking term to describe money that you've added to your account.

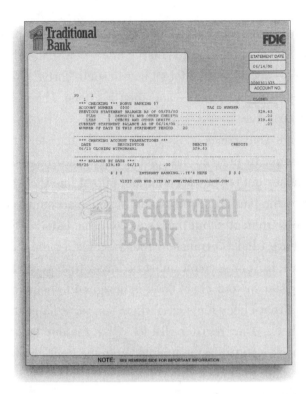

The bank statement includes directions on the back that explain exactly how to know what your balance is at the current moment. That's in case you've written a check or made a deposit since the bank mailed your statement. *Balancing your checkbook* is the phrase used when you double-check the statement's record of all checks, deposits, and fees charged to your account. You should end up with the same amount of money that the statement says you have, minus any unrecorded deposits or plus any checks that have not yet cleared or been deducted from your account.

ACCOUNT BALANCING SECTION

_____ 1. Enter Ending Checking Balance from the front of this statement.

_____ 2. Enter deposits (credits) not shown on this statement.

_____ 3. Sub-Total (add line 1 and line 2).

_____ 4. Enter total of checks (debits), fees (if any), and automatic payments entered in your register, but not shown on this or previous statements.*

_____ 5. Balance (line 3 minus line 4). This amount should agree with your register.

LIST OF OUTSTANDING CHECKS & WITHDRAWALS

CHECK #	CHECK AMOUNT	CHECK#	CHECK AMOUNT

*TOTAL (LINE 4)

Practice Writing Checks

Practice filling out checks with these pretend checks. Write a check to Mascot Jackets for $93.27. Be sure to fill in every line on the check with the required information. Record your check in the register on the following page. Now write a check to Lofty Top Shoes for $41.33 and fill in the register. Pretend you had a balance of $393.17 in your account when you began. Be sure to subtract each check from the balance in the register and enter in the new balance. How much money do you end up with after writing these two checks?

525

73-151/421

DATE

Pay to
the order of _____ $ _____

_____ DOLLARS 🔒 Security features included. Details on back.

🏛 **Traditional Bank**
MOUNT STERLING, KENTUCKY 40353

FOR _____ _____ MP

⑆042101514⑆ 00311375⑈ 0525

526

73-151/421

DATE

Pay to
the order of _____ $ _____

DOLLARS 🔒 Security features included. Details on back.

🏛 **Traditional Bank**
MOUNT STERLING, KENTUCKY 40353

FOR _____ MP

⑆042101514⑆ 00311375⑈ 0525

NUMBER	DATE	DESCRIPTION OF TRANSACTION	PAYMENT/ DEBIT (-)	√ T	FEE (IF ANY) (-)	DEPOSIT/ CREDIT (+)	BALANCE $	
		RECORD ALL CHARGES OR CREDITS THAT AFFECT YOUR ACCOUNT						

REMEMBER TO RECORD AUTOMATIC PAYMENTS/DEPOSITS ON DATE AUTHORIZED

Debit Cards

Although lots of people use paper checks (especially to pay bills), more and more people have turned to a plastic version of a check. When you open a checking account, most banks offer you a check card, which is also called a *debit card*. It's called those things because you can use your card in place of a check to withdraw money from your account, or "debit" your account. Just like checkbooks, debit cards are a little safer than cash. If you lose cash, it's just gone. If you lose your debit card, no one else can use it because you have to have a special number, like a secret code, to use it. It's called a *personal identification number*, or PIN. You even get to choose your own PIN number so it's easy to remember.

Another thing about debit cards is you can use them to deposit money into or take cash out of your checking or savings account even when your bank is closed. You do this at an automated teller machine, called an ATM, at any hour, day or night. ATMs are located almost everywhere: in malls or grocery stores, on the sides of buildings, even in bank lobbies. You just follow the easy directions on the screen of the ATM to put in your PIN and make your deposit or get your cash. At the end you get a receipt that shows the balance on your account.

Comparing Credit and Debit Cards

Now let's look at plastic money called credit cards and compare them to debit cards. Credit cards work like this: when you buy something and pay with a credit card, you promise the store that you will pay for your purchase at the end of the month. Actually, you are promising the store that a bank will pay for it at the end of the month. When you buy something with a credit card, a bank will pay for your purchases even if you don't have any cash in your pocket.

But there's a hitch: many banks make you pay a fee each year for the use of their credit cards, and a bigger hitch is that if you don't pay off your credit card bill in full each month, the bank charges you an extra fee for using their money. These fees can add up the longer you don't pay your balance. It's like paying more for items that, maybe, you bought on sale in the first place. Sadly, you can get into financial trouble with credit cards. This is because credit card companies sometimes give you a line of credit (the total amount you can charge) that is far higher than you can afford to pay off easily. So even though credit cards have benefits, like not having to carry around a lot of cash, they have some dangers too. In 2008, almost 78% of American households—91.1 million families—had at least one credit card, and that number is expected to grow.

When you buy something with a debit card, the amount of your purchase is immediately subtracted from the money you have in your bank account. Instead of writing a check, you simply hand the cashier your debit card and the amount of the purchase will be automatically subtracted from your account. All you have to do is sign your name on the store's copy of the receipt and enter the amount of the purchase in your check register in order to keep track of how much money you have left in your account.

When you use a debit card, you don't have to worry about paying fees—unless you buy things that cost more money than you have in the bank. When you spend more money than you have in your account (either by writing checks or using your debit card), it is called an *overdraft*. When you overdraft, the bank makes you pay a special fee. That fee may be bigger than the check you wrote that put you over your limit in the first place! People who keep track of the amount of money they have in the bank usually don't overdraft. Since you already know how to use your check register to enter not only all the checks you write but also all the purchases you make with a debit card, your cash withdrawals or deposits at an ATM, and the deposits you give to a teller at your bank, you won't make the mistake of overdrafting on your account.

A word of caution about credit cards: a lot of parents will not let their kids have credit cards if they are under 18. They are right to do that, because overspending on a credit card can cause a big financial mess. When you reach college age, however, credit card companies are quick to find you. They bombard you with offers to use their plastic money. At first they offer you a low interest rate to lend you money upfront for purchases you want. But in six months or a year that interest rate will change, and it almost always goes up, not down. If you pay off your credit card bill in total each month, it will not matter what the interest rate is. Unfortunately lots of people don't do that. Then you get stuck with paying more interest each month on a balance that grows bigger and bigger whether you buy anything at all. That's why a lot of college students graduate not only with student loan bills but with big credit card bills as well. You can compare rates and services for credit cards at www.creditcardguide.com or www .cardratings.com. (Recent legislation protects card users who are under 21; a cosigner or proof of employment is required.)

Billy Ray Buys Some Money

Billy Ray Fawns bought money by exchanging it for something he owned and by exchanging it for a skill. Billy Ray was born in 1977 and grew up in Mount Sterling, a town in central Kentucky with a population of about 5,200 people. Billy Ray's father is a bricklayer who owns his own business. Billy Ray says, "He worked hard for the money to support our family."

Billy Ray started making money in kindergarten and first grade by selling the fruit his mother packed in his lunch. He sold his banana or apple for a dollar. (Can you believe it?) He doesn't know how he got the idea to sell his fruit in the first place. This went on until he asked his mother if she would put two pieces of fruit in his lunch box. When she guessed what was going on, she put a stop to the fruit-for-money exchange. This didn't keep Billy Ray from selling his old tennis shoes to a classmate for $15.

Billy Ray also worked for money. When he was 11 he fell in love with a motorcycle that cost $2,000. His father told him that if he worked all summer helping with bricklaying jobs, he would match the money that Billy Ray saved. So Billy Ray, who was big for his age, worked and saved his money. He worked all summer, carrying bricks and mixing mortar and doing almost anything the bricklayers needed. In the evenings he mowed yards and did other odd jobs for people. At the end of the summer he had saved half the price of the motorcycle. His dad kept his promise and Billy Ray bought his cycle. But he realized something that summer—working that hard for his money taught him to respect it. And he realized something else—he wanted to figure out other ways to make money.

In this chapter you learned

- how to buy money,
- how money is made,
- how money circulates,

- how to write checks and use debit and credit cards,
- and how to keep track of the money you have in the bank.

If you only remember one thing about money, though, it should be this: money changes hands over and over, and at some point you may decide to try to stop the circulation of your money long enough to save some. But even when you think you're taking money out of circulation by saving it, you can still get paid for doing this. That's where our investment story really begins.

Two

All About Saving

HOW TIME AND A LITTLE MATH CAN MAKE YOU RICH

Savings Accounts

THERE ARE A number of ways to save money. You can hide it in your room, bury it in the garden, or ask a friend to keep it for you so you won't spend it in a moment of weakness—but none of these ways is really safe. You may lose it in your room if you haven't picked up your clothes lately, your dog may think you were burying a bone and dig it up, and your friend might forget that it is your money and spend it on herself. One of the best places to save money is in a bank. That's what banks do—they keep money for people. At least, that's part of what they do.

A bank is a place that stores money for you and lets you have it back when you want it. They protect it too. But instead of making you pay to guard your money, the bank pays you for keeping it in one of their savings accounts. A savings account is like a checking account, except you can't write checks. Banks pay you because they let other people borrow money from you. What you get from the bank, in exchange for letting your money be used and loaned to others, is more money. Your money is also protected by a very strong insurance policy.

This is how it works. You ask the bank to keep your money in a personal savings account. Just as you do with a checking account, you have a savings account number that identifies your money. Your friend George also has a savings account in the same bank, and so do George's parents, your parents, and the guy who cuts your hair. They all put money in their personal savings accounts in your bank. The bank now has a lot of money that it's keeping for everyone, separated by the different account numbers that belong to each of these people.

Soon after you opened your savings account, your math teacher, Ms. Henderson, decides she wants to buy a summer home on a golf course. So she walks into the bank and asks to borrow some money to pay for the house. The bank says, "Sure, you can borrow money. We've got a lot of it. But you have to pay us a fee every month while you use our money." Ms. Henderson says OK and pays the bank to borrow the money. The bank then turns around and pays you part of the money Ms. Henderson paid them. After all, your money is part of the money she borrowed. The money they pay you is called *interest,* and the interest adds up and up. This is how the money you save makes even more money.

Banks are not the only places that like to guard your money and then pay you interest for this right. Credit unions also help you save; in fact, they were created about two hundred years ago to make it easy for farmers and other workers to borrow and save money. Credit unions work just like banks—with two big exceptions. First, they are nonprofit organizations. This means that instead of trying to make a lot of money for the people who own stock in the bank (you'll learn about stock in the next chapter), the role of credit unions is to make money for their members. Second, credit unions don't have to follow the rules and regulations set by the Federal Reserve that all banks in the United States are required to follow. (Chapter

6 will explain how the Federal Reserve works.) Instead, credit unions follow rules set by the National Credit Union Administration (NCUA).

Credit unions are owned by the persons who use them. They are kind of like a club that you belong to where you all have something in common, like living in the same neighborhood, going to the same church, or working for the same company.

There's a very important rule that credit unions have that is different from banks: the credit union board members, who are sort of like school principals, decide how much they pay members like you to take care of and to lend out your money. Banks pay interest based on the rate the federal government thinks is best. Credit unions set their own interest levels. They can pay as much as they want. Also, because credit unions are non-profit companies, any profit they have at the end of the year is given back to the members who save there. So credit unions are worth checking out for your savings accounts, as they can offer higher interest rates than banks. You might even get a bonus interest payment at the end of the year.

Money Market Accounts and Certificates of Deposit

There's another easy way to save money: you can put your money in a money market account. A money market account is a savings account with a boost. You sign up for money market accounts through banks or investment companies. Money market accounts give you a little more interest than a straight savings account, because the money in the accounts is invested for you by people who are trained to make investments. The investments are safe ones, plus you can write checks against the money in your account. There are certain rules, though, like checks you write have to be at least $500 or some other pretty big amount. You also have to pay the bank that holds your account a small portion of the money it makes for you for this service. The majority of the time, even after subtracting this fee you usually still earn more money than in a savings account.

There's one more way to save money. You can buy a certificate of deposit, or CD, from your bank. (Not all CDs play music.) CDs are for savers who won't need a certain amount of their savings for the next six months or year or two years. When you buy a CD, the bank pays you a little more interest than it pays for savings accounts or money market accounts. The longer the period of time of the CD, the greater the interest you get paid. If you decide you won't need $500 for the next two years, and you buy a two-year CD, you will earn more interest than if you buy a six-month CD. There's a hitch though: if you take out your money before the term of the CD is up, the bank will charge you a penalty. Then you will lose money instead of making it. There's a good reason you make more money with CDs. It's better for the bank when you promise that it can use your money for a longer length of time. This is why a bank will pay you more interest on a two-year CD than on a six-month CD. This is also why the bank charges you a penalty fee if you cancel your CD early, because your money has already been lent to other people to buy houses, cars, boats, and other expensive things. Although banks used to be the only place to invest in a CD, credit unions also provide them. It's worth checking out because credit unions often provide higher rates of return on your money.

Here's how it stacks up. You are paid a certain amount of interest on a savings account; for banks, that amount is pretty much determined by the government. (I'll explain how this amount is determined in chapter 6.) You earn a little more interest if you put your money in a money market account at either a bank or a credit union. You earn a little more interest still if you purchase a CD, especially if it is a one- or two-year CD.

Remember, you can shop for the best interest rate just as you or your folks shop for the best price on a new car. A good place to do that is online. At www.e-wisdom.com, you can check out all sorts of things including savings rates, CD rates, and credit card services and fees. For a comparison on bank rates on all types of accounts, go to www.bankrate.com. To do the same comparison with credit unions, go to www.creditunionsonline .com. If you want to explore a site of a single credit union, try out www .msfinancialfcu.org. For a single bank site, go to www.northerntrust.com.

The Power of Compounding

Knowing different places to put your savings is just half of what it takes to make money. The other half—and in some ways the most important half—is understanding time and the power of compounding.

You can earn interest in one of two ways. One is called *simple interest* and it is, in fact, simple to describe. Simple interest means that you will get a certain amount of interest for a determined amount of time. For example, you may be told that if you open a savings account with $100 and keep it in the bank for one year, you will earn 6% interest. That means you will earn $6 at the end of the year ($100 × 0.06 = $6). That would give you savings of $106 for the year ($100 + $6 = $106). That's simple interest.

The other kind of interest is called *compound interest*. Compound interest has a lot to do with time. Here is where a little math comes in. Remember when I said at the beginning of this book that if you saved $8,000 a year between ages 7 and 21 and left it in the bank earning an average of 4.50% a year, you would have $1 million at age 65 without ever saving again? Well, that's the power of compounding. When interest is compounded, banks pay you interest on the interest you've earned for each day or month you have money in your savings account. Here's how it works: You open a savings account with $100 in a bank that pays 6% compound interest. The bank will say it pays 6% annual percentage rate, or APR. You divide this rate over 12 months to get the monthly interest rate. In this example, that's 6%, or 0.06, divided by 12 months. That equals 0.005 interest a month, and 0.005 times 100 equals $0.50. Add that to your $100, and at the end of the first month you have $100.50. The next month the bank pays you interest not just for the $100 you originally put in, but also for the money (50 cents) it paid you to keep it there. At the end of the second month you have $101.00, and so on until at the end of the year you have $106.17.

That's the power of compounding. It's like magic, except there are no tricks. You just sit there and watch it happen month after month and year after year. If your $100 had earned simple interest at the same 6%, you would have made $6 over the year. You may think that 17 cents is not much difference, but just imagine if you had $500 in your savings account, or $1,000. The difference between simple and compound interest increases as you put more money into your account. Your original $100 will keep compounding, and by the end of 5 years you'll have $134 (instead of $130 from a simple savings account) and at the end of 10 years you'll have $179 in your account (instead of $160).

$100 at 6% Interest Compounded Monthly			
Month 1	100.50	Month 7	103.55
Month 2	101.00	Month 8	104.07
Month 3	101.51	Month 9	104.59
Month 4	102.02	Month 10	105.11
Month 5	102.53	Month 11	105.64
Month 6	103.04	Month 12	106.17

There are a number of sites online that will calculate the money you will save over time in your savings account. Just make sure you are using a compound interest calculator and not one for simple interest. A useful site is www.csgnetwork.com/compoundsavingcalc.html. Another site that allows you to add to your initial savings each month is www.calculatorweb .com—with this site, you can see how much money you would have in the future based on a savings plan. For example, if you start with $100 at age 8 and add $20 a month for 10 years, you would have a little more than $3,100 when you graduate from high school.

Compare Interest Rates at Banks and Credit Unions

Do a search for different banks and credit unions. You can look online or around town. Select three. Find out what interest rates the institution offers on its savings accounts. If you are walking around town, there may be a sign in the bank window that reads something like "3.25% APR." Make sure you know whether the interest rate is simple or compound. Note that when you compare rates online—at www.e-wisdom.com or www.bankrate.com—there is a code that tells how frequently your savings compound, such as "D" for daily or "M" for monthly. Copy the table on the next page to record the information you gather.

One month later, check out these places again to find the interest rate. Fill in the date and the new interest rate. Is it the same or has it changed? If it has changed, try to figure out why. The chapter on the economy (chapter 6) will help you do this. Which place offered the highest return last month? Which one this month? Is it the same?

Name of Bank or Credit Union	Contact Number or Web Site	Account Type: Savings (S) or Money Market (MM)	Interest Type: Simple (S) or Compound (C)

Date of First Check	Interest Rate at First Check	Date of Second Check	Interest Rate at Second Check

Saving money is the first step to investing. In the beginning, it seems hard or even impossible when you think of the CD—that's *compact disc*—that just came out or that great cashmere sweater your best friend bought on sale. But once you start saving, it's hard to stop, because you see your savings grow as the bank or credit union pays you interest every single month. You begin to dream of how much more money you'll have the longer you wait to spend it. You may even become so enthusiastic that you'll add even more of your allowance, babysitting money, or part-time job salary into your account.

$ Calculate Your Interest Earnings

This activity will show you how to figure out how much money you'll have in a savings account in one year if you have money to set aside.

Go back to the list of interest rates you collected from banks and credit unions in the previous activity. Pick an amount of money that you would like to save. Take the dollar amount you've chosen and the interest rate the first bank will pay you. Use the math and example on page 24 to help figure out how much you would have from each of your three banks or credit unions in one year. Remember that even small amounts of interest add up over time—that's the power of compounding.

Calculate Your Interest Earnings

Annual Interest Rate/12 = Monthly Interest Rate

Savings Amount
× Monthly Interest Rate + 1

Savings Plus Interest Earned for One Month

Here's an example. You have $200 to open an account. Bank A is offering an annual interest rate of 5% on its savings accounts. It requires a minimum initial deposit of $200. This is how you calculate your interest earnings:

1. Change 5% into a decimal number (0.05).

2. Divide .05 by 12 to get the monthly interest rate (0.00416).

3. Calculate your savings at the end of month 1 by adding 1 to the monthly interest rate and multiplying by your savings amount ($200.00). Your result should be $200.83. Repeat this step using the new savings total for each month.

4. Calculate a couple more years until you understand this calculation. Copy the table below to organize your information. Now calculate your interest earnings using the bank rates you collected in the previous activity. Create tables like the one here to organize your information and make it easier to compare banks and their rates.

$200	5% Interest Rate
Month 1	$200.83
Month 2	$201.63
Month 3	$202.44
Month 4	

Bank Name:	Bank A
Annual Interest Rate:	5%
Amount Needed to Open a New Savings Account:	$200

Some Things You Should Know About Interest Rates

Interest rates change over time. You may have noticed that each of the examples I have chosen to illustrate simple and compound interest has a different interest rate. That's because interest rates change from year to year and even from month to month. Chapter 6 will explain why this happens. For now, it is important to know that when you begin to save money, time will be part of the equation. Consequently, savers should not think just in terms of current interest rates but also of interest rates over time. At any given moment, economists who look at historic interest rates might say that the average interest rate over the previous ten years was 6%. Looking forward they may estimate that over the next ten years the interest rates will average 5%. That means that some years the interest rate may be as low as 1% and in some it will surpass 7% or 8%. When you start to save, keep in mind that, historically, when interest rates are low, it is likely that they will go higher over time; when interest rates are high, it is just as likely that they will come down.

Billy Ray felt the magic of saving. When he was eight his parents started a savings account for him with a gift of $500. From that time on, whenever he received birthday or Christmas money, he deposited it into his savings account. He didn't buy many toys, as his friends did when they were given some money. He was having more fun wandering around outside and practicing basketball. So he just tucked his money away.

One day he realized that the more money he had in his savings account, the more quickly it seemed to grow. He didn't know anything about the power of compounding at that point, even though in school he had done those math problems in which Mary has $100 and she puts it in a bank and earns 5% interest. Somehow he never thought about those problems as real life. They were just homework.

Billy Ray woke up to this reality when he began watching his savings account grow—faster and faster—and it made him want to save more. Whenever he cut grass or shoveled snow, he put half of the money into his savings account and kept half for his own spending money. He called it "paying himself." As he watched the money accumulate in his savings account, he began to try to figure out how to make his money grow even faster.

One day, just like Billy Ray, you will look at your total savings and be shocked by how much you have. That might also be the moment you think to yourself, "I wonder if there's a way to make even more interest than I'm getting now." There is. That's when you become an investor.

In this chapter you learned

- about savings, money market accounts, and CDs;
- how to calculate compound interest;
- and the secret of time and how it earns money.

What you don't know yet is how personalities fit into the investing picture. You'll learn about this in the next chapter.

All About Investing
HOW TO MAKE MONEY MAKE MORE MONEY

Risk Tolerance

NOW IT'S TIME to get down to the heart of the matter—making money. You have a little money saved and you like the feeling of watching it grow, but you'd like to make it grow faster. Are there ways to make more interest on your money than by keeping it in a bank or savings and loan? Yes! This chapter is all about how you can make your money make more money— that is, how to invest your money. You will learn how to spend some of your savings to make a little more money on something called an *investment*. If you follow one of these strategies for making money that I'll detail here, then you will be an investor.

Investing is not just about spending and making money. It's about time and personality types. When people talk about investing, they use words like *compounding* (which, if you remember, has to do with time) and phrases like *risk tolerance* (which has to do with personality type). Both of these factors are important. Compounding was covered in the last chapter, so now it's time to think about risk tolerance, especially your own.

Risk tolerance has to do with how people approach life. You know from watching family members or friends that some people are afraid to try new things. They are afraid to try activities like playing lacrosse, taking dance lessons, or going to the mall by themselves. On the other hand, there are some people who don't seem to be scared of anything. These are the people who are the first to answer advertisements for jobs during the holidays or over summer vacation, even though they've never worked for anyone in their lives. They are also the ones who will raise their hands in class even if they're not sure they really know the answers. Some people are a combination of both extremes. In fact, most people are combinations, but they tend to be more one way than the other. That has to do with their personalities. Neither way is good or bad—it's just one of the ways that people differ.

The way people tend to act and the things they tend to worry about in their lives show their risk tolerance for investments along with everything else. Some people are afraid to lose their savings, so they will be very careful when they invest. They might just leave their money in a savings account and never invest at all. These people have a low risk tolerance. Others are willing to take a chance to make a lot of money, even if it means they might lose some of their savings. They have a high tolerance for risk.

You are the only one who knows what you will feel comfortable doing. You might even have to try a riskier investment or two before you know for sure. But whether you have a low or a high risk tolerance, there are investments available for you.

$ Make a Risk Tolerance Chart

Make a list of 10 of your friends or family members. Think about the things they do and the way they behave. Observe the behavior of each person on your list for a while. Does one of your friends dislike being called on in class even when he has his homework done and knows the right answer? Does your sister like biking, hiking, and other exciting activities? Note if the person likes adventures, if he tries new things, or if she speaks up in class often.

Make a chart like the one pictured here. This chart will help you keep track of the levels of risk tolerance for your 10 friends and family members. Divide your chart into 12 rows and 4 columns. Write your friends' and family members' names in the first row of the far left column. In the first row of the next column, write "Does Not Take Chances." In the first row of the third column, write "Sometimes Takes Chances." In the first row of the last column, write "Loves to Take Chances." Place an X in the box that you think best describes each person after you've had some time to observe them. In the first column of the last row, write in your name and place an X in the box that best describes your behavior. Ask your friends where they'd place you on this risk tolerance scale. Did they tell you exactly what you marked down for yourself? Get their feedback on how you charted the other people on the list. Do you agree or disagree with their opinions?

Name	Does Not Take Chances	Sometimes Takes Chances	Loves to Take Chances

Bonds

United States Savings Bonds

Now that you know about risk tolerance, it's time to think about what investments to make. The two most common investments are stocks and bonds. Bonds are investments that have less risk and therefore are good investment choices for people with low risk tolerances. Bonds are a good, steady investment. They earn money for you on a regular basis, with hardly any risk that you will lose your money. That's why bonds feel comfortable to investors with a low risk tolerance. Bonds help you make more money than bank, credit union, or money market accounts pay you.

What exactly is a bond? A bond is an agreement between you and another party—think Intel, Ford Motor Company, or even the United States of America—stating that the party can use, or borrow, your money for a set period of time. It can be three months, six months, one year, two years, five years, or even twenty-five years. In return for letting this other party use your money, it will pay you just as a bank pays you, but it will pay you more than the bank does.

Just as banks will pay you to save money, the federal government will too. The federal government is the United States government (which differs from your state government), or, as some older people say, "Uncle Sam." (Uncle Sam is big with grandparents.)

Grandparents, aunts, uncles, and friends of the family like to buy U.S. Savings Bonds to give as gifts on birthdays and holidays. But anyone can buy savings bonds—even you.

The most popular savings bond is called the Series EE bond. You can purchase this type of bond for as little as $25 or as much as $10,000. Savings bonds are pretty interesting because what you are really doing is letting Uncle Sam—that's the United States of America—borrow money from you! Here's how it works: The U.S. government sells savings bonds. When you buy one, you are saying to the government, "You may use my money for a certain number of years." It can be as few as 5 years or as many as 30 years. You give the government some of your money—say $50—and in a few years (based on the current interest rate) the government gives you back $100. The difference between the $50 and the $100 is your interest, just like from a bank or credit union. But this time, you have the government's IOU. It's a fancy piece of paper that looks kind of like money—that's the bond.

At the end of the time of your loan, the bond "reaches maturity," which means the time period of the bond has expired and you can now collect the face value of the bond. (Since you paid much less than the face value, the difference is your profit!) When the bond reaches maturity, you can take it to any bank. The bank gives back the amount of money you lent the government, plus what it agreed to pay you for the loan. What you get back is your investment return. (*Investment return* is another way of saying *interest earned*.) For more information on savings bonds, go to www .treasurydirect.gov. You can also find out the current interest rate on U.S. Savings Bonds by calling (800) 4US-BOND, or (800) 487-2663.

There are many kinds of bonds besides savings bonds, but there are only three that you need to know about right now. They are called *treasury bonds*, *municipal bonds*, and *corporate bonds*. You may not want to buy any of them yet, but you need to know about them for when you get your first real job or if you make a lot of money on your investments before then.

$ Search for a Savings Bond

Go on a savings bond search. Ask a parent if you or anyone in your family has ever received a savings bond. Then ask your friends if any of them was ever given a savings bond. Try to see one in person. It might be locked in a safety deposit box for safekeeping. If you can't find an original, go to www.treasurydirect.gov/instit/savbond/mat/ clipart/clipart_savbond.htm to check out what the different denominations look like. They are pretty impressive.

Treasury Bonds

Treasury bonds—or *treasuries*, as they are usually called—are IOUs from the federal government (Uncle Sam again). Treasuries are really just bigger savings bonds. Sometimes the government runs out of money just when it needs to pay for something; and just as you might ask your best friend if you can borrow a little money until your next allowance, the U.S. government asks you if it can borrow from you.

When you buy treasury bonds, you are lending money to the government. To prove that you lent it money, the government gives you an IOU. The IOU is a contract with a promise to pay you back at the time you agreed on. The key is that you are paid back with interest. Sometimes the interest is paid back at the end of the contract and sometimes it is paid along the way.

There are different names for the lengths of time you lend the government money. These are

- *treasury bill* (less than 1 year),
- *treasury note* (1 to 10 years),
- and *treasury bond* (more than 10 years).

You should buy treasury bonds through a mutual fund group when you first start to buy them. (Mutual fund groups are covered later in this chapter.) You can buy them in smaller denominations if you buy them this way. *Denomination* is just another word for *amount*. Although you can buy treasuries for as little as $1,000, the standard denominations are $10,000 for individual investors and $100,000 for banks and brokerage firms.

Municipal Bonds

Another kind of bond is a municipal bond. They're interesting because so many of the things you see and use every day may exist because of municipal bonds, such as your school, a hospital, a bridge, or even a nearby jail. The water that comes out of your faucet may get to your home because of a municipal water bond. This might also be true for your electricity—it might come from an electric power bond.

Cities or towns—and even counties and states—are officially referred to as *municipalities*. That's why bonds that help pay for schools or hospitals are called municipal bonds. When a town or a city wants to build a new school, parking garage, or hospital, they often ask the people who live there (and even people who don't) to lend it some money to finance or pay for the project.

The people who agree to lend money to the city—or municipality—get an IOU. They invest in the city's project. The city then agrees to pay the investors money—usually every six months—for letting it use your money. The amount of interest paid is based on the length of the loan. Investors who agree to lend their money for five years are paid a higher interest amount than those who will lend the city money for only one year. If you agree to let the municipality use your money for 30 years, the interest is even higher.

At the end of the contract, the municipality gives back the full amount of the loan. The original amount that you let the municipality borrow is called the *principal*. (This principal is not the top dog at your school, even if it's spelled the same way.) But don't forget that even before you get your principal back, you have been paid every six months to let the municipality borrow your money.

The thing that's especially nice about municipal bonds is that you can look at structures in your own hometown and know you helped build them. Another really nice thing about them is that you usually don't have to pay taxes on the money you earn while your money is on loan. That's not as important to you right now as it is to your parents. (I'll talk more about taxes in a later chapter.) One last thing: since municipal bonds sell in pretty big denominations, it's best to buy them through a mutual fund. This way you can invest as little as $500 or $1,000 in a group of municipal bonds. Otherwise you would have to buy one bond for $5,000, the usual denomination size.

Corporate Bonds

Finally, you should know about corporate bonds. Corporate bonds are similar to treasury and municipal bonds. The only difference is the borrower. Rather than lending money to the government or a municipality, people who invest in corporate bonds lend money to a private company for a private purpose. Corporate bonds are fun because you can lend money to companies you know, such as McDonald's, Apple, Google, Nike, or the Gap.

When you invest in corporate bonds, you let companies use your money to expand. Sometimes this might be to build a new cafeteria or pave a second parking lot; other times it may be to update the company's computer equipment and wiring. Your money may even make it possible for the company to build a whole new plant. The company believes that the improvement it wants to make will increase its profitability, and it will be able to pay you back with interest out of its increased profits.

Corporate bonds pay a little more interest than treasuries or municipal bonds. That's because there is a little more risk involved. Companies are businesses and they exist because people buy what they sell. If you and your friends and many other people stopped buying this company's products, then the company could go out of business. Needless to say, when a company goes out of business, it is not making the money it needs to pay back investors.

Bond Market Risk Rankings

When you invest in the bond market—that's lingo for when you buy bonds—you have a low level of overall risk. But there are different degrees of low-level risk among these various bond products. The risk ranks like this, from the lowest to the highest: government bonds (those are savings bonds and treasuries); municipal bonds (those are bonds of cities, counties, and states); and corporate bonds (those are bonds of companies like Kellogg's or Pepsi). Still, even when you invest in corporate bonds, you do not have the level of risk you have when you buy stocks, as you'll see in a minute.

$ Discover What's Built by Bonds

Walk or ride your bike around your neighborhood or town and look for things that might be built by bonds, such as schools, hospitals, and parking garages. If there is a large plant in your town, like a car manufacturer, for example, it was probably built by bonds. Ask your principal if the school was built with municipal bonds. You might have to explain what a municipal bond is, but you can do that.

If you can get to a hospital, ask the receptionist or person at the information desk to direct you to whomever can tell you if the hospital was built with municipal bonds. Again, you may have to explain what a municipal bond is. You may also have to explain why you want to know. Just say it's for an investment project you're working on. Keep asking until you find the right person. You will probably have some interesting conversations with these people, especially if you end up talking to the director of the hospital. It will be an adventure, one that you'll talk about with pride.

Stocks

It's time to move on to stock. What is stock anyway? *Stock* is the amount of money a business company is worth. There's a special term for the money in a business—it's called *capital*. So another way to define stock is to say that stock is the capital of a business company. Some companies, like car manufacturers, have huge amounts of capital. Other companies, such as start-up technology firms, have smaller amounts of capital.

Imagine a company as a huge pie. The pie is the company's stock. Now picture the pie cut into 100 pieces. Each piece of the pie is a share of the stock. Sometimes a company decides to sell some of its stock. It lets the public—that's us—buy pieces, or *shares*, of the pie. (In fact, when a private company sells its stock, it's called "going public.") When you buy a share of stock, you become part owner of the company—you become a shareholder.

A company that goes public usually wants to keep the biggest part of the pie for itself. That's in case some of the shareholders don't agree with the way the company is being run. There can be big arguments at shareholders' meetings, where people yell and scream at the people who manage the company. But the shareholders with the most shares get the most votes, so if the company that sold the stock in the first place owns the most shares, it can do what it feels is best.

A company may decide to sell different kinds of stock shares to the public. They can sell common or preferred shares. A *common share* is a regular type of share that most people have. A *preferred share* is one with extras, such as being one of the first stockholders to be paid dividends if there's a money crunch. The difference is sort of like the difference between hot fudge sundaes with whipped cream and nuts and hot fudge sundaes without them. Also, there might be Class A and B shares—there might even be Class G and H shares. Each type is slightly different than the other, but those differences are not so important to you now. All you need to know is that they exist. The most common type of stock to buy is the common share. Makes sense, doesn't it? Common shares are the type you will start with because they are simple and there are more of them than other types.

Buying stock in a company is different from buying bonds in the same company. When you buy a bond, you are lending the company money and it will pay you back with interest. When you buy stock, you are buying a piece of the company and no one has to pay you back if money runs short. You are an owner. Your return depends on the strength of the company.

If you can't be sure you'll get your money back, why would you even consider buying stock? The answer is that you have a chance to make more money with stock than with bonds. As an owner, if the company makes a lot of money, you get part of it—a part equal to the size of the piece of pie, or number of shares, you own. The possibility of making a big return on your investment is why people are willing to risk some of their savings with stock purchases. Whether you can handle that possibility has to do with your risk tolerance.

When you buy stock, you sometimes get the benefit of stock splits. If a company is doing really well, the price of a share usually goes way up. This is because a lot of people want to buy shares in a successful company and few shareholders want to sell when their investments are doing so well. It's like when you have something that someone wants to buy, but you really like it and you won't sell it unless you get a lot more money than you paid for it. When the price of a stock goes up so high that a lot of people can't afford to buy a share, the company will sometimes do a stock split— it will split your shares in half or in thirds. This means you will have two or three shares for every share you owned before the split. This does not mean, however, that you suddenly have two or three times the amount of money you did before the split. That's because the price of each share is also cut in half or thirds. But after the split, the price of your shares usually continues to go up. Then you have more money than you did before the split, because now you own more shares.

Keeping Track of Your Stock

When you're a shareholder, the company sends you information about what it's doing. Shareholders get reports in the mail every three months or so. These reports are really just report cards, like those you get in school. In the case of stocks, the report tells you what the company has accomplished since it last contacted you. Once a year you get a report about what happened during the whole year. The report includes a written statement from the president of the company and information about how much money the company made for the year, how much it spent, and how much was left over to give to the shareholders (that's you).

The reports from the company help you figure out if the investment is living up to what you expected. Then you can decide if you want to keep your shares, sell them, or buy more shares. It boils down to the answer to this question: Are you making enough money to take the risk of owning stock? If no, then sell. If yes, then hold (that's a market term that means "stay with what you have"). If yes big-time, then buy more.

It's time to mention risk tolerance again. People who invest only in stock need to have a higher tolerance for risk than those who invest only in bonds. That's because there is a greater chance of losing money with stock than there is with bonds; but at the same time, there is a greater chance of making money. Each person has to decide what she is comfortable doing with her savings. As I'm sure you've heard a thousand times, you have to try something before you know whether you like it.

The key to stock investments is that you can make more money when you take bigger risks. Lion tamers make more than circus clowns, and high steel construction workers make more than carpenters because there's more risk. It's the same with investments. You will make more money with stocks than you will with bonds because there's more risk.

Find a Stock Report

Find a stock report. A quick way to do that is to ask your parents if they own any stocks or stock funds. If they do, ask to see one of the company's annual reports. If your parents don't own stock or mutual funds, ask your grandparents. If that doesn't work, try searching online. Type in the name of a company that you might be interested in, followed by "annual report" (for example, "McDonald's annual report"). Choose a company you are familiar with, one whose clothes you wear, whose cell phone you talk on, or whose food you eat. When you find a report, look it over to see the various sections and different kinds of information the report includes. Read the president's report. You don't have to understand every word. Can you tell from this report if it was a good year for the business? Do you find any evidence in the report itself to back up what the president's report claims? The goal is just to know what an annual report of a business company looks like, but if you can also understand some of the information, that's even better. After reading the report, would you buy stock in this company?

Mutual Funds

There's another way to invest your money—you can buy shares in a mutual fund. A mutual fund is a company that invests money for you. Mutual funds come in many different varieties. In fact, there are more than 5,000 mutual funds available. There are mutual funds that just invest in treasury bonds. There are funds that just invest in municipal bonds and ones that just invest in corporate bonds. There are also funds that invest in stock companies. There are mutual funds that only invest in companies that have been around for a while, like John Deere, and there are funds that just invest in newer companies, like Google. There are mutual funds that invest in big companies and funds that invest in small companies. Almost anything you can think of that has to do with investments has a mutual fund of its own. The important thing for you to know about mutual funds is that you don't have to be a big investor to buy shares in one.

This is how a mutual fund works: One or two people pick out a group of stocks or bonds

There are a lot of words that investors use to mean *investment earnings. Return*, as in *steady return*, is similar to the word *interest* (which means the money you are paid for the use your money). *Return* refers to the money you earn on an investment. *Yield* is another one. You will hear statements like, "My fund returned 10%." Or, "The yield on the fund was 10%." Both sentences mean the same thing. I guess it's just like the words *sweet, the bomb, cool, awesome,* and *phat*—they all mean something's great.

to go into a mutual fund that has a specific investment goal. The goal of the fund might be to make a lot of money quickly, or it might be to invest money for a steady return—that means you can be pretty sure you'll get your money back with interest. The group of stocks or bonds that go in the fund is called a *portfolio*. The one or two people who pick what stocks and bonds to buy and sell are called *portfolio managers*.

Portfolio managers pick out a group of stocks or bonds that meet a certain goal and then they sell you shares in it. You already know that treasuries come in big denominations. Well, municipal bonds do, too—usually $5,000 a bond. But if you buy shares of a mutual fund, you can invest in treasuries or municipal bonds for as little as $1,000. What you are doing is buying a part (a share) of a treasury bond or a municipal bond. After you make your first purchase, you often can invest as little as $25 at a time in a mutual fund.

Besides making it easy for you to invest in a group of stocks or bonds, mutual funds cut down the risk of investing in stock. Here's how: When you buy shares in a mutual fund, you buy a tiny part of each of the stocks or bonds that the portfolio manager has put in the fund. If one of the stocks or bonds doesn't pay off as you had hoped, you won't lose all of your money. You will lose only a tiny part, as long as all the other stocks or bonds in the fund are still fine. For example, say you bought a fund that invested just in soft drinks like Coca-Cola, Pepsi, 7UP, Canada Dry, and XYZola. XYZola has some problems. It goes bankrupt and the fund loses a little money, but all the other soft drinks are selling like crazy. You consequently did not lose all your money. In fact, you only lost a small portion of your money. What mutual funds do is help you to diversify your risk. "To diversify" simply means to spread out your risk. It's like when you play dodgeball—the more people who play, the less risk there is that you'll be the first one out.

On the other hand, if you had purchased shares in XYZola alone and it went bankrupt, you would have lost your whole investment. Gone. That's a good reason why you should invest in some mutual funds at this stage in your investment career. You should still invest in stocks. Just don't put all of your money into just one.

$ Think of Ways to Earn Money

Write down five ways that you could earn money. Think about all the things you are good at. Perhaps you already have a job like babysitting or are paid by your family for jobs you do around the house. If not, make a list of some of the things you do well. Are you an organizer? Can you do big jobs like cleaning out the basement or the garage and then run a yard sale? Or do you like pets? Could you be a dog walker or work for a veterinarian who would pay you to clean out cages and feed the animals on weekends? Use your imagination.

Next, follow up on at least one idea. First, check with an adult in your house. He or she might have some task that needs to be done right away. Put the money you earn aside in case you need to buy supplies (for example, a lawn mower if you decide to mow lawns or car wax if you decide to wash cars).

Work down the list. The job you find may not be your first choice, but just think how much fun it will be once you have enough money to invest.

Billy Ray Invests in Himself and Starts a Small Business

Billy Ray was good at basketball, so instead of getting a full-time summer job while he was in high school, he went to basketball camp. He still did odd jobs, but mostly he practiced basketball. His family saw it as an investment in Billy Ray's college education. This investment paid off. Billy Ray went to Georgetown College in Georgetown, Kentucky, on a full basketball scholarship and never had to take out a student loan to help pay for his education.

Remember that Billy Ray had been paying himself when he did odd jobs during the school year, tucking half of that money into his savings account. In the early spring of his sophomore year in college, when he was

19, Billy Ray decided he had to do something with his summers to earn more money to save.

Winter has always been his brainstorming time. He says his mind works best when it's dark outside. So he started talking to people about jobs. One of those people he talked to had supported himself in college by starting a lawn-mowing company. Billy Ray decided that was a good choice for him, too.

He did some research to find out the things he needed to do to start his company.

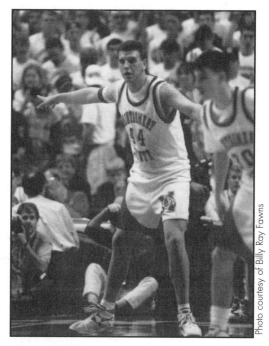

The Legend

Billy Ray found used equipment in nearby Lexington. His dad bought him a trailer to haul a mower, a weed eater, and a blower. He figured out how many lawns he would have to mow and then how many months it would take to pay for the rest of the equipment. Next, he went to the bank—the same one where he had saved his money since he was eight. He asked the bank for a small business loan to buy the equipment he needed. He explained his lawn-mowing business idea and how he planned to pay the bank back. He filled out the loan forms; the bank reviewed them and decided to give Billy Ray the loan. He was off and running.

Billy Ray figured it would take a full year to pay off the loan. He paid it off in two months. During this period, the number of people who wanted him to mow their lawns increased, and he realized he needed better equipment. So he went back to the bank and got another small business loan. He paid this one off the first month of his second summer. Now he owned his equipment free and clear. That meant that everything he made from mowing from then on was profit and could be invested. He had the money; now he just needed to learn how to invest it.

In this chapter you learned the major ways investors invest and grow their savings. You learned about the following topics:

- risk tolerance
- savings bonds
- treasuries and the different types of treasury bonds
- municipal bonds
- corporate bonds
- stocks
- mutual funds
- risk levels of each type of investment and the investment choices best suited to you, depending on your level of risk tolerance

Now it's time to find out how you actually make an investment and where you go to do it.

All About the Market

WHAT IS *THE MARKET*, AND WHERE IS WALL STREET?

Wall Street

Now that you know what shares of stock are, it's time to talk about where you buy them and what you do when you get there. The place to start is on Wall Street.

The history of Wall Street is almost as interesting as the history of money. Wall Street is located in New York City, at the southern end of the island of Manhattan. Manhattan is one of the oldest parts of the city. You've probably heard the story about how it was purchased from the Lenape Native Americans in 1626 for the equivalent of about $24. Peter Minuit, a Dutchman, gave the Native Americans who lived and hunted there a few bead necklaces and trinkets in exchange for the land.

But there's another part of the story that you don't usually hear about. That's about the Dutch giving New York, or New Amsterdam as it was called then, to the English. Well, they didn't exactly give Manhattan to the English. They actually traded Manhattan to the English for a tiny island called Run Island, located in the East Indian Ocean near Indonesia. Run is so tiny that hardly anyone knew how to get there—except the Dutch and the English who had fought over it for years. Run was worth its weight in gold because of a special tree that grew there—a nutmeg tree. Although now nutmeg is used mostly in cakes, cookies, and Swedish pancakes, back then it was used for medicine. Everyone wanted nutmeg. So not only was the island of Run worth its weight in gold, it was also worth Manhattan to the Dutch, who gave it up in the Treaty of Breda in 1667.

Wall Street is a short street in the oldest part of Manhattan. It was named for a wall. A fortress was built near the edge of the island, and outside the fortress wall was a buttonwood tree. As early as 1792, people started meeting under this tree to trade shares of stock. Pretty soon more and more people were meeting under the buttonwood tree. Finally they couldn't all fit, so they met anywhere along the street by the fortress wall. Because Wall Street was so short, stock traders that got there late had to meet under other trees, on the curb in front of buildings, or anyplace else they could find. Before long the whole area around Wall Street was called Wall Street, no matter what street traders met on. Now, "Wall Street" means New York's financial district, where investors buy and sell stock.

Stock Exchanges

Trading shares of stock doesn't take place under buttonwood trees or on curbs anymore. Instead it takes place in buildings and is done through companies called *stock exchanges* or *stock markets*. These companies are like huge supermarkets where you can buy, sell, or exchange almost any-thing—sort of like a Super Target or Super Walmart. Although there are numerous stock exchanges and stock markets around the country—including exchanges in Boston, Chicago, Los Angeles, and Philadelphia—the main ones are on Wall Street.

New York Stock Exchange (NYSE)

The most famous of the Wall Street exchanges is the New York Stock Exchange. Originally it was called the Buttonwood Group (because of the investors who met under the buttonwood tree). Now it's often referred to by the letters "NYSE." The NYSE is the major place where investors go to trade shares of big, established companies that make products like cars, stoves, refrigerators, computers, and cameras.

The floor of the NYSE—where stocks are bought and sold—used to be one of the noisiest places in America. It was amazing to watch the traders yelling and screaming and jumping up and down, trying to be sure someone saw that they were buying or selling something. Just imagine a basketball tournament, with all the noisy fans and cheerleaders from both teams. Now things are quieter, because every trader has his or her nose in a computer.

National Association of Securities Dealers Automated Quotation (NASDAQ)

There is also a market for companies that make things like medicine, computer software, and other technological inventions. This market is called the NASDAQ Stock Market. NASDAQ stands for "National Association of Securities Dealers Automated Quotation." It's a long name, but all you need to remember is "NASDAQ," which rhymes with "has Mac."

Investors can buy or sell stocks electronically on the NASDAQ exchange from anywhere in the world. In fact, investors who trade through the NASDAQ were probably the first of the online shoppers. Although the NASDAQ has more stocks listed for trade than the NYSE, the NYSE is still considered the granddaddy of the stock exchanges.

In late December 1999 and early January 2000, the NASDAQ opened a video tower and studio in Times Square in New York City. The tower is the largest video screen in the world. People can stand on the corner of Broadway and 43rd Street and watch news events and get information about the stock market all day long if they want. The NASDAQ's MarketSite Studio is a broadcast studio with 96 video screens to help reporters with their market update broadcasts. Since the tower is glass, you can also watch everything that's going on in the building. Find a TV channel that gives business news. If the reporter is standing in front of a lot of screens with charts, she is probably at the NASDAQ studio.

Over-the-Counter Market (OTC)

There's one more market that you should know about. It's called the over-the-counter market, or OTC. It really isn't a market like the big three markets. It's more like a flea market or a yard sale. It's for all the stocks that are too new and too small to be listed on one of the major exchanges.

The name for over-the-counter trading comes from an actual process. Originally, stock certificates were traded by handing them over a counter in a firm where brokers bought and sold stock for investors. Now the OTC market should be called the over-the-phone or over-the-computer market, since that's the way most of these tiny stocks are traded. In fact, some of the newer company stocks are so small that they are traded for pennies a share. If you have heard about "penny stocks," the OTC market is where you usually buy them.

Some stocks trade over the counter so infrequently that it's hard to find out anything about them. There used to be two places where you could get information on what it costs to buy or sell one of these new or inexpensive stocks. Originally, the National Quotation Bureau (NQB) put out lists of stocks that were too new or too small to be registered with the Securities and Exchange Commission (which will be covered later in this chapter). In 2000 NQB joined forces with the other list for OTC stocks: Pink Sheets. Pink Sheets, which once printed its lists on pink paper, is now published electronically. At www.pinksheets.com, you can click on a guide to the over-the-counter market, as well as check lists of stocks available for purchase. Try it. Eventually, you may want to check into penny stocks for your investment portfolio.

Visit a Stock Exchange

Now that you know there are stock exchanges in New York City and other major cities, it's time to visit one. If you live in New York, arrange a visit to the NYSE—or you can just go to the corner of Broadway and 43rd Street and watch the NASDAQ video that shows current stock prices. If you visit the NASDAQ MarketSite Studio, you can play an interactive investing game or walk through the Information Tunnel to see what the global stock market is like.

If you live in Boston, Chicago, Los Angeles, or Philadelphia, visit the exchanges in these cities. You might do this with your parents, or perhaps you could talk your teacher into planning a field trip to one of the exchanges. Each exchange has a viewing area, and most of them offer guided tours.

Here is contact information for the stock exchanges in New York and Chicago:

New York Stock Exchange (NYSE)
11 Wall Street
New York, NY 10005
(212) 656-3000
www.nyse.com

NASDAQ MarketSite Studio (NASDAQ)
4 Times Square
New York, NY 10004
(212) 728-8333
www.nasdaq.com

The Chicago Stock Exchange (CHX)
440 North LaSalle Street
Chicago, IL 60605
(312) 663-2222
www.chx.com

The Chicago Board Options Exchange (CBOE)
400 North LaSalle Street
Chicago, IL 60605
(312) 786-5600
www.cboe.com

If you don't live near any of the cities mentioned above, search the Internet for videos of the stock exchanges.

The Market

Now that you know what stock exchanges are, it's time to learn how they work. The stock market is a lot like your local soccer league or a major baseball league. There are teams, players, and rules. To have a good season, everyone has to work together.

Here's how it happens: First, there are the stock exchanges, which are like sports leagues. These exchanges are where the shares of stock are traded, just as team members are sometimes traded to other teams. Then there are the brokerage houses or firms, which are like team owners. Each firm is an investment company that is a member of the stock exchange. The brokerage firm pays the stock exchange to have what it calls "a seat" on the exchange. When a brokerage firm has a seat, it can buy or sell stocks through the exchange.

Each brokerage house hires stockbrokers, sometimes just called "brokers." They are the players. Brokers are trained to advise investors about the best stock or bond buys and to take care of either buying or selling stock for you on the stock exchange. Just like major league players, the best brokers get the biggest salaries.

The process of buying or selling the stock is actually called "writing a ticket." When you buy a ticket to a baseball game, part of the cost of the ticket goes to the team owner to cover the costs of owning a baseball team and part of it goes to the player in salary. The same thing happens with brokers' commissions—part of the commission goes to the brokerage house to cover costs and the rest goes to the broker in salary. The broker who writes the most tickets makes the most money.

The Birth of the Dow

In 1884, Charles Dow, a young journalist working in New York City, decided to make a list of 11 stocks that traded on the New York Stock Exchange. He thought that the 11 he picked, such as railroads and manufacturing companies, reflected America's wealth. Each day he wrote down the closing price for a share of each of the stocks, added them all together, and divided them by 11 to get the average. Sometimes he even published his list.

Before long, Dow joined forces with Edward Jones, another journalist who, like Dow, reported on business news. The two of them founded the *Wall Street Journal*, which regularly published this list called the Dow Jones Industrial Average (DJIA) or "the Dow." The *Wall Street Journal* is now the most important business newspaper in the United States—and maybe the world. Every day this business newspaper publishes a list of stocks and their average prices. The DJIA is used around the world as an indication of the strength of America's stock market. The stocks in the Dow are not the same ones that Charles Dow started with, and more have been added since it began—but the concept is still the same. The Dow still follows big, well-established companies like Boeing, Coca-Cola, Disney, and McDonald's. These stocks even have a nickname: "blue-chip" stocks, named for the poker chips with the highest value.

The Securities and Exchange Commission (often referred to as the SEC or "the Commission") sets the rules for the stock and bond markets. Think of the SEC as the baseball commissioner. The SEC makes sure the broker tells you everything you need to know to make a reasonable investment decision and then sends you a stock receipt on time. If the broker doesn't send your purchase documents to you or mishandles your purchase, the SEC investigates the reasons and sets penalties. If a broker is in trouble with the SEC, she may not be able to make stock or bond trades anymore. Plus she may have to pay a huge fine—hundreds of thousands of dollars—and even go to jail. A number of brokers were tried and jailed in 2008 and 2009 for lying to their clients about stock trades.

The Scoreboard

There's an easy way to check a scoreboard for the stock market each day—it's by looking at the ending numbers for the Dow Jones Industrial Average, the NASDAQ Composite Index, or the Standard & Poor's 500. There are other stock indexes, like the Russell 2000 Small Stock Index, but the Dow Jones Industrial Average, the NASDAQ, and the S&P 500 are the ones you hear about most often.

The word *average* is probably familiar to you. You hear it in school a lot, as in "grade point average" or "average reading scores for the eighth grade." You also know sports terms such as a "batting average" in baseball. These are quick ways to compare students or athletes. The term *index* is another word that gives you a quick way to make these comparisons, such as comparing today against yesterday or a year ago. The Dow Jones Industrial Average shows how 30 stocks of large, well-established companies, like Coca-Cola or Caterpillar, that trade on the New York Stock Exchange sold for the day. It tells you whether the value of a group of stock shares went up or down.

All the indexes work the same way. They measure share prices with different types of stock. The NASDAQ Composite Index gives a quick look at new companies and technical stocks, like Intel Corporation or Apple. The Russell 2000 follows small companies that you have probably never heard of. The key is that when you hear the Dow mentioned on the news as "going up" or "dropping" a certain number of points for the day, it indicates that the stock market gained or lost value.

The Internet makes it easy to check out the various exchanges. Just search for "Dow Jones Industrial Average," "DJIA," "NASDAQ," or "stock indexes," and you will find all you need to know. For an overview of the different types of stocks, go to www.stockmarketinvestinginfo.com/smi _stocktypes.html.

Find a Stockbroker

Before we get to the next section that tells you how to place a stock order, you might want to see if there are any stockbrokers in your community. Search online for "Stock and Bond Brokers" to find listings for brokerage houses, like Charles Schwab or Fidelity. Many stock sales are handled through electronic brokerage houses like TD Ameritrade or E*TRADE. To compare costs and services of electronic brokers, check out www.fool.com/how-to-invest. The site will also provide guidelines for electronic investing. You can also look up stockbrokers in the phone book.

How to Place a Stock Order

To be able to play any kind of sport, you have to understand how the game works. You also have to know the meanings of the words that the coaches and other players use. The same is true with investing. I'll review a few important terms for you, so that at the end of this chapter you'll know how to place an order.

When you call a broker or go online to buy or sell stock, you "place an order." There are a number of things you need to know before you make that trade:

- The name of the stock you want to buy or sell
- The class of the stock and whether the stock shares are common or preferred
- How many shares you want to buy or sell
- What you will pay or want to be paid for a particular stock (called *setting the price*)

The first three things are pretty straightforward. The fourth thing, however, means you have to know the lingo.

The simplest way to set the price, and the way most people do it, is to place a market order. A *market order* means that you will buy or sell your stock at the current market price. It's the same as going into a store to buy a pair of jeans. You walk straight to the shelves, find the style and size you want, and walk to the checkout counter to pay for them at the price marked on the sales tag. You want the jeans, you buy them, and there's no wait. It's the same way with stocks—if you place a market order, the trade is finished almost at once.

There are, however, two other ways to place an order. You can place a stop order or a limited order. Both orders set limits on the price you are willing to pay (buy) or will accept for (sell) your stock. A stop order tells the broker to buy or sell a stock the moment the market price hits the price you set. A limited order is similar to a stop order, but there's one difference. A limited order allows the broker to sell your stock at an even better price than you indicated, if someone offers more than you expected; also, if you can buy it at a lower price than you were willing to pay, then the broker can save you money on your original order.

Here's how it works. You decide you want to purchase 10 shares of DigitalU stock, because you always have to wait in a long checkout line when you purchase something there. This personal experience tells you that DigitalU is a popular place. You look online and find not only that DigitalU traded for $10 a share yesterday, but also that over the last 52 weeks it has sometimes traded as low as $8 a share. (I'll explain how to check this out in the next chapter.) You decide that you are willing to buy the stock at $9 a share. You ask the broker to place a stop order to buy 10 shares of DigitalU stock at $9 a share. If you are under the age of majority, which is eighteen in most states, an adult will have to make your stock purchases. If that's the case, you may have to tell them what to say. When you place either a stop or limited order, the broker will ask if you want a day order or a good-till-canceled (GTC) order. If you answer that you want a day order, the order will be open until the stock market closes trading on that very day. If you answer that you want a good-till-canceled order, your order will be open until it's filled or until you cancel it. To "fill an order" simply means to buy or sell the stock you want. So, if your order is filled, it means you bought 10 shares of DigitalU at $9 a share. You then pay the broker $90 (10 shares × $9), plus the broker's commission.

You sell stock shares exactly the same way. Let's say that your Teentech.com stock has spiked up and down over the last year. You bought it at $18 a share and the stock has traded as high as $26 a share. When you check online, you see that yesterday the stock traded at $20. You decide to sell your shares if you can get $22 a share. So you place a stop order with the broker to sell all of your Teentech.com shares when the stock hits $22 a share. You also tell the broker that your order is good for 30 days, which means that you are willing to wait 30 days to see if it sells. If Teentech.com does not reach $22 a share in 30 days, the broker will contact you and ask if you want to cancel your order or keep it open. Then you can decide if you want to keep the stock or place a GTC order. It's that simple. Just as you're comfortable with the terms *strike*, *out*, and *safe* in baseball, soon you'll feel the same way about the terms *market*, *stop*, and *GTC orders*.

How to Place a Mutual Fund Order

Mutual funds are made up of individual stocks, but placing a mutual fund order is a lot easier than placing a stock order. The main reason is that you don't have to know any terms except *buy* and *sell*. To place an order for mutual funds, you call the mutual fund company that manages the fund you want. All you have to say is, "I want to buy $500 of your MYScene Fund," or, "I want to buy 50 shares of your MYScene Fund," which means the same thing. The person who takes the call will ask if you have an account with the mutual fund company. If this is your first purchase, she will mail you a short form to fill out. You send it back with your check or money order to purchase the stock, and it's done. The mutual fund family will even send you a form that lets you add money—say, $25—to your fund whenever you want. All you have to do is send the form back with a check or money order made out to the name of the fund. When you want to sell, you just call the fund company and say you want to sell a certain amount of your fund. You can do this in dollar amounts or in number of shares. It's as easy as that. In a few days, you will receive a check in the mail for what you sold.

You can also buy a mutual fund online. If you do it this way, you follow the prompts on your computer to make a purchase. Most fund companies have simple directions because they want to make it easy for you to invest your money with them. As with any investment, if it's your first time with the fund company, you will have to fill out some paperwork.

There are good reasons for buying mutual funds. I've described some of the reasons in chapter 3. Some people, though, buy mutual funds only because they don't know how to place a stock order. They are afraid they'll sound dumb if they don't know exactly what to say. But you already know what to say, so you can buy either stock or mutual funds based on which is the best investment for you. Besides, you don't have to worry about what other people think. Remember, you're the one with the money to invest.

Write a Script

Write a script for a stock order. Pretend that you're going to buy 10 shares of stock in the company that makes your favorite shoes. Write out two scripts for the person who will place your order: one for placing a market order with a broker and one for placing a stop order. Finally, write out another script—while you write this one, pretend that you already own stock in the shoe company and you want to sell your shares. Decide if you want it to be a stop or limited order and adjust your script. Decide if you want it to be a day order or a GTC order and add this information to the script too. For a good primer on stock investing, go to www.stockmarketinvestinginfo.com.

Billy Ray Plans to Invest

Billy Ray thinks through each of his decisions carefully. He figured that in the second summer of his mowing business he'd be able to save most of what he made. So he started going around and asking adults, "Looking back, if you were my age, what would you do with your money now that you didn't do then?" He listened carefully to what everyone had to say and collected all the information. He researched different types of investments that were mentioned, made his decisions, and formed a plan.

He decided to divide his savings into thirds—one third was for high-risk investments, one third was for medium-risk investments, and one third was for low-risk investments. He figured out which investments were best for him, and then he made his move.

In this chapter the stock market was introduced to you. You learned

- that the history of Wall Street began under a buttonwood tree;
- how the market works;
- that there are different stock exchanges;
- that when investors buy or sell stock, they contact a stockbroker;
- that stockbrokers work for a brokerage house, and the brokerage house is a member of one or all of the stock exchanges;
- and how you can get a quick look at how well stocks did for the day by looking at the Dow Jones Industrial Average.

Next you'll learn how to research the stocks you're interested in.

All About Stock Tables

HOW TO READ THEM FOR FUN AND MONEY

How to Read Stock Tables

YOU KNOW THE terminology and how the market works, but before you actually place an order, you have to decide what you're going to buy. This is the next step in the investment process. It's kind of like a detective game. You try to learn all you can about a stock from just a few clues. After you learn how to read the clues, picking the right stock becomes a piece of cake.

57

The good news is that these clues are at your fingertips—you can find them on your computer or in newspapers and financial publications like *Barron's* or *Money* magazine. There you will find all the information you need in lists of stocks called *stock tables*. Reading stock tables is something that lots of people don't know how to do, and many are scared to even try. By the end of this chapter you'll be able to show your friends how to do it. Before you go any further, look up a stock table online. One place to do this is at www.investopedia.com/university/tables/tables1.asp. Explore the site to get an overview. Also check out www.stockmarketinvestinginfo.com/smi_stocktypes.html, which gives an overview of the stock market. Although it may look confusing at first, once you know what to look for, it will make sense. After you've read this chapter, go back to the two sites and see if it all makes more sense.

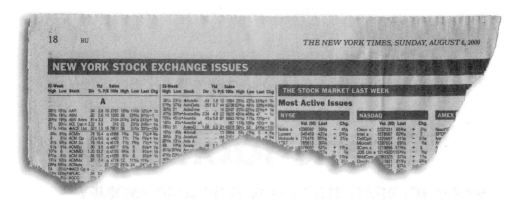

A stock table tells you the recent history of a stock, just like statistics on the sports page tell you how well a baseball player has done over the season. There are two main reasons you need to understand these tables: (1) to see how the stocks you own are doing and (2) to see how stocks you might want to buy have done in the past. This will help you decide if you want to buy shares in a particular company. There's actually one more good reason to learn how to read the stock tables: so you'll never be afraid to use them. If you aren't afraid, then you won't be slowed down when you have money to invest. It's like learning how to ride a bike—once you know how to do it, you never even have to think about it again. You just get on and ride. The only difference is that learning to read stock tables is a lot easier than learning how to ride a bike.

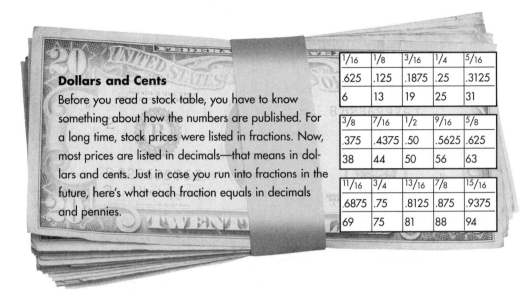

Dollars and Cents

Before you read a stock table, you have to know something about how the numbers are published. For a long time, stock prices were listed in fractions. Now, most prices are listed in decimals—that means in dollars and cents. Just in case you run into fractions in the future, here's what each fraction equals in decimals and pennies.

$1/16$	$1/8$	$3/16$	$1/4$	$5/16$
.625	.125	.1875	.25	.3125
6	13	19	25	31

$3/8$	$7/16$	$1/2$	$9/16$	$5/8$
.375	.4375	.50	.5625	.625
38	44	50	56	63

$11/16$	$3/4$	$13/16$	$7/8$	$15/16$
.6875	.75	.8125	.875	.9375
69	75	81	88	94

Here's an example. Let's say that you hear on television that Disney has made a new film that will open around the holidays. You think Disney might be a good stock to own, but you don't have a clue about what it costs per share. The quickest way to find out is to check the stock tables. Either do it online or visit a library or bookstore that has financial publications.

The Walt Disney Company

Since the Walt Disney Company is a large company, I looked first for the stock—both in the paper and online—under the list of stocks that trade on the New York Stock Exchange. And there it was, as NYSE: DIS. If it had not been there, I would have looked under the NASDAQ National Market. If you are looking online, the quickest way to find Disney, or any stock, is to go to www.marketplace.com or http://finance.yahoo.com and enter the name of the stock. Notice in the illustration from the financial publication that the stocks are listed alphabetically and that across the top of each table are headings in dark letters for each column. Reading them from left to right they are: "52-Week High, Low, Stock," and so on. Most publications have a box inserted somewhere near the stock tables that explains what each of the headings means. Online services often include

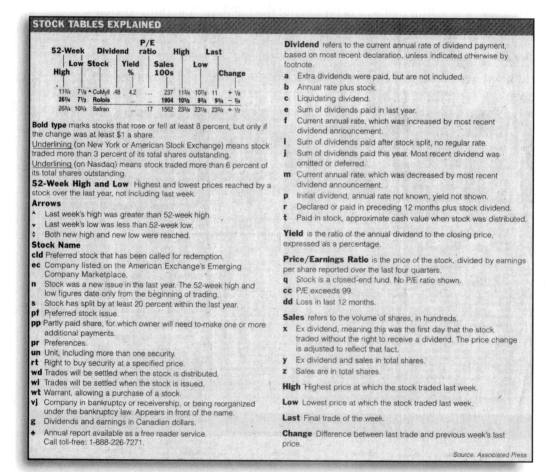

STOCK TABLES EXPLAINED

52-Week High	Low	Stock	Dividend	Yield %	P/E ratio	Sales 100s	High	Low	Last	Change
11¾	7⅛ ▲	CoMyll	.48	4.2	...	237	11¾	10⅞	11	+ ⅛
26¼	7½	Rolois	...	...	...	1904	10⅝	9¾	9¾	− ¾
26¾	10¾	Safran	...	...	17	1562	23¾	23⅛	23¾	+ ½

Bold type marks stocks that rose or fell at least 8 percent, but only if the change was at least $1 a share.

Underlining (on New York or American Stock Exchange) means stock traded more than 3 percent of its total shares outstanding.

Underlining (on Nasdaq) means stock traded more than 6 percent of its total shares outstanding.

52-Week High and Low Highest and lowest prices reached by a stock over the last year, not including last week.

Arrows

▲ Last week's high was greater than 52-week high.

▼ Last week's low was less than 52-week low.

↕ Both new high and new low were reached.

Stock Name

cld Preferred stock that has been called for redemption.

ec Company listed on the American Exchange's Emerging Company Marketplace.

n Stock was a new issue in the last year. The 52-week high and low figures date only from the beginning of trading.

s Stock has split by at least 20 percent within the last year.

pf Preferred stock issue.

pp Partly paid share, for which owner will need to make one or more additional payments.

pr Preferences.

un Unit, including more than one security.

rt Right to buy security at a specified price.

wd Trades will be settled when the stock is distributed.

wi Trades will be settled when the stock is issued.

wt Warrant, allowing a purchase of a stock.

vj Company in bankruptcy or receivership, or being reorganized under the bankruptcy law. Appears in front of the name.

g Dividends and earnings in Canadian dollars.

✦ Annual report available as a free reader service. Call toll-free: 1-888-226-7271.

Dividend refers to the current annual rate of dividend payment, based on most recent declaration, unless indicated otherwise by footnote.

a Extra dividends were paid, but are not included.

b Annual rate plus stock.

c Liquidating dividend.

e Sum of dividends paid in last year.

f Current annual rate, which was increased by most recent dividend announcement.

i Sum of dividends paid after stock split, no regular rate.

j Sum of dividends paid this year. Most recent dividend was omitted or deferred.

m Current annual rate, which was decreased by most recent dividend announcement.

p Initial dividend, annual rate not known, yield not shown.

r Declared or paid in preceding 12 months plus stock dividend.

t Paid in stock, approximate cash value when stock was distributed.

Yield is the ratio of the annual dividend to the closing price, expressed as a percentage.

Price/Earnings Ratio is the price of the stock, divided by earnings per share reported over the last four quarters.

q Stock is a closed-end fund. No P/E ratio shown.

cc P/E exceeds 99.

dd Loss in last 12 months.

Sales refers to the volume of shares, in hundreds.

x Ex dividend, meaning this was the first day that the stock traded without the right to receive a dividend. The price change is adjusted to reflect that fact.

y Ex dividend and sales in total shares.

z Sales are in total shares.

High Highest price at which the stock traded last week.

Low Lowest price at which the stock traded last week.

Last Final trade of the week.

Change Difference between last trade and previous week's last price.

Source: Associated Press

the same information, but they do not always explain the terms. Since it's important for you understand the data, here's what each heading means.

52-Week High: The highest price that was paid for a share of stock in the last year (52 weeks). Sometimes you'll see an arrow pointing up in the "52-Week High" column. That means that the selling price listed for the current day is the highest in the last 52 weeks.

52-Week Low: The lowest price that was paid for a share of stock in the last year. Sometimes you'll see an arrow pointing down in the "52-Week Low" column. That means that the selling price listed for the current day is the lowest in the last 52 weeks.

Stock: The name of the stock. If the company name is short enough, like Disney or Benetton, then the full name is used. If the company name is long, like Barnes & Noble, then a shortened version is used. Barnes & Noble's shortened version is BarnNbl. Like this one, the abbreviations of other companies' names are usually close enough that you can find them.

Sym: The company stock symbol. Some papers include a column for the stock symbol and some papers don't. Companies try to make their symbols close to their actual name (like OAT for Quaker Oats), but if there are a lot of names that are similar, then sometimes the symbols don't match up so well. If you're really curious but can't figure out the meaning of an abbreviation, then you can call one of the brokers you found in your community or check it out online.

Div: The dividend, or the estimated amount that you will get per year in cash for each share that you own. If there is a blank under the "Div" column, it means the stock does not pay a dividend. (In this case, your investment return comes from an increase in the price of the stock.) Dividend is sometimes called *yield*. Remember that *interest*, *dividend*, *yield*, and *return* all mean money earned.

Yld %: Percent yield. This is a clue about dividends. The percent yield tells you the dividend percent based on the price paid for the stock. In the case of Disney, the company expects to pay a dividend of .21, or 21 cents per share. On the day I'm using for the newspaper example— August 6, 2000—Disney sold for 42 $7/16$, or $42.44 a share. (Use the conversion table on page 59 and round to the nearest penny.) If you divide .21 by 42.44, you get 0.0049. (When you are dealing with percentages, you move the decimal point two numbers to the right. You end up with 0.49 or, rounded up, 0.5, which is what the stock table shows. Don't worry—you won't ever have to do this calculation yourself. I just wanted to explain how the table got this number. I knew someone once who worked through all of Einstein's calculations on relativity just so he would know for sure how it was done. It took him a year. But don't panic, because you won't ever have to do that either.) Now take a look at the price of a share of Disney stock on December 31, 2009, in the online example on page 59. You will use this for an interesting exercise at the end of the chapter.

P/E: The price to earnings ratio. This means the price divided by earnings. The price part of the equation is the price that the stock last sold at. The earnings part is the amount the company earned per share over the last year. The stock table does not supply us with the amount of earnings the company had over the previous four quarters or full year. The table simply gives the P/E ratio. What it tells you is how expensive, or "pricey," the stock is compared to what the company earned during the last year. It's sort of like paying $50 for a ticket to an unknown music group when you could see the hottest group around for the same price. The closer the price is to the earnings the better, so look for lower P/E ratios.

Sales 100s: The amount of shares that changed hands on the last business day. The number is given in hundreds, which means you add two zeros to the end of the number to see exactly how many shares sold. Sometimes the heading is "Vol 100s." That means the same thing. Here's a weird little twist: if there is a Z in front of the number, you don't have to add the zeros. If you see "1522" in the "Sales 100s" column, that means 152,200 shares sold; but, if you see "Z1522," it means that only 1,522 shares were sold. If there is a line under the stock's entry, it means that more shares than usual changed hands, and that usually means that there's some important news about the stock.

High: The highest price paid for a share of stock for the day. Remember, the high on the left side of the table is the high for the year. If it's on the right side, it's the high for the previous business day.

Low: The lowest price paid for a share of stock for the previous business day. Again, the low on the left side of the table is the low for the whole year.

Last: The price of the last share sold for the previous business day. Sometimes this heading is "Close," which means the "closing bell price" and, consequently, the last price. This is usually the first column investors look at to see what their stock was worth at the end of the day. You'll hear it referred to in a number of ways, such as "closing price" or "market close."

Chg: This column gives you the amount of change ("Chg") between the previous day's closing price and the closing price from the day before that. There will always be a plus (+) or a minus (–) sign in the "Chg" column to tell you whether the stock went up or down. (See the table for the meanings of other abbreviations.)

Disney from Start to Finish

Now let's look at Disney from start to finish. (Refer to the stock table on page 59.) You hear about this new movie coming out for the holidays and you want to see if you can afford to buy some Disney stock now. You also want to get a picture of how the stock has done over the last year, so you go online or find a financial publication and check the New York Stock Exchange.

Using the newspaper example in the book, you look over to the right side of the columns—the column for "Last"—to see what the stock price was at the end of the previous day. You see that it closed at 42 $7/16$, or $42.44 a share. You then check the next column to the right to see if it closed up or down from the day before. In this case, it was up 4 $9/16$, or $4.56 over the last day. That's good in one way. It means a lot of people think Disney is a good stock. But it's bad in another way, because you would rather pay less for the stock than more. If you had bought it on the day before the current listing, you would have saved more than $4.50 a share.

Now you look all the way over to the left edge of the table and you check to see what Disney's high and low prices have been for the last year. In the last 52 weeks, Disney shares sold for as low as 23 $3/8$, or $23.38, and as high as 43 $7/8$, or $43.88. Going back to the closing price on our table, you can see that Disney is currently selling near its high for the year. That's not so good. It means that Disney stock is pretty expensive right now. It also means that everyone who heard about the new film had the same idea as you, so all of them are buying the stock. You check the number of shares that sold in one day and you see that more than 36 million shares were sold. That's a lot of shares. (When a lot of people want the same thing, it means the seller can ask more because someone out there will want it badly enough to pay a higher price.)

The next question to ask is what kind of dividend you could expect to earn in a year for each share of stock you purchased. You see on the stock table that you would get 21 cents a share. So if you bought 10 shares, which would cost you $424.40 at the listed price, you would get about $2.10 in earnings for the year (10 × .21 = $2.10). Now you ask yourself how that dividend compares to other stocks. Disney's dividend compared to the stock price is 0.5%, which is low. If you look at the stocks above and below Disney, you see that most of them have a higher dividend percentage. One stock even gives dividends that are equal to 13.4% of the cost of a share of stock. Then you look at the P/E ratio—how much the price of a share is compared to the earnings for the last year. You see that Disney stock is selling for 85 times the amount of earnings the company made per share over the last four quarters. That's not good. That's too high.

Now you have the tools to make a decision. The decision to buy or not is often a hard one. It's hard because often your heart wants to do one thing and your head tells you something else. You would love to tell your friends that you own some shares of Disney stock. Then, each time Disney released a new film, you would feel really proud because you owned a part of the company. However (and this is the hard part) Disney stock is selling near its highest price in 52 weeks, and its dividends are low compared to the price of the stock. Plus, what you would have to pay for the stock compared to the amount of money the company earned last year is too high. This means that Disney is not the best buy right now. So, even though you had a good idea when you heard about the new Disney film, and even though you would love to own some Disney shares, it's not a good investment.

Some investors just buy what they want without doing their research, but that's like betting on a horse just because you like its name. Those horses rarely win. You'll come out a winner much more often if you do the research first and then make your decision based on what you find.

Pat yourself on the back, because you now have more than half of the tools you need to call yourself an informed investor!

$ Look Up Stocks

Look up the following stocks online or in a financial publication: Nabisco, the cookie company; United, the airline; and Microsoft, the software company. Check all three exchanges to find these stock listings.

Now look up Disney. In the chart below, first add the numbers from the online entry for Disney from December 31, 2009. Then fill in the information you have found for the current date.

Disney Stock Value Over Time											
Date	52-Week High	52-Week Low	Stock	Div	Yld %	PE	Sales 100s	High	Low	Last	Change
Aug 2000	$43 \frac{7}{8}$	$23 \frac{3}{8}$	Disney	.21	0.5	85	360736	43	38	$42 \frac{7}{16}$	$+4 \frac{9}{16}$
Dec 2009											

Compare the three sets of numbers and ask yourself the following questions:

- Does a share of Disney stock cost more or less today than it did in August 2000 and December 2009?

- What happened to the highs and lows? Have they changed a lot or are they pretty much the same as before?

- Has the dividend changed?

- Has the P/E ratio gotten better or worse? (Better means the ratio is lower; worse means it's higher.) Remember that the price to earnings ratio gives you a comparison between the price of the stock and the company's last years' earnings. If the P/E ratio is high, it means you are paying a lot for a stock that has low earnings.

- What about sales? Is the stock still as popular as it was in August 2000?

- Finally, would you have made money if you bought Disney stock in August 2000? Has the price gone up, down, or is it about the same?

You just did a stock analysis! When you look up a stock in the stock tables, it gives you a picture of the stock for one day. It's a snapshot. When you check a stock once a week or once a month, you can see what a stock does over time. The kind of comparison you just did with Disney—looking at the stock over time—is closer to a video than a snapshot portrait of a company. This is exactly what brokers and financial advisors get paid to do every day. Did it ever occur to you that you could do it too?

Go tell someone over age 18 some of the things you've just learned or show him or her how to look up a stock in the paper. You can use Disney if you want, since you know exactly where to find it. Do the same analysis for the other three companies: Nabisco, United, and Microsoft. Are any of these better investments than Disney at this time? When you can explain what you know to someone else, it means you have really learned it.

Reading Mutual Fund Tables

Now that you know how to read stock tables, you'll be able to read mutual fund tables too. They're very similar. However, to make certain that you're as comfortable reading the mutual fund tables as the stock tables, I'm covering them separately here.

Remember that a mutual fund is simply a group of stocks or bonds selected by a portfolio manager. Investors buy shares in the fund, just like they do in a single stock. When you buy shares in a mutual fund, you own a part of each of the stock companies in the fund. Also remember that mutual funds help you spread out your risk. (Refer to chapter 3 if you need to review this information.)

As you can see from the following graphics, funds are listed under bolded names. This is the name of the investment company that manages the group of funds listed beneath it. The funds that a company manages are referred to as its *family of funds*. Each fund has a different investment objective. Some have low-risk levels and some have high-risk levels; some give you big dividends, and some don't give any dividends at all.

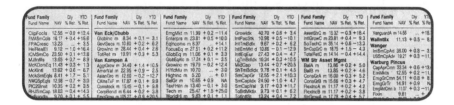

When you check on mutual funds in a financial publication or online, you see just a few columns:

Fund Family: The name of the company that manages the mutual funds in its list.

Fund Name: Placed right below the "Fund Family" heading, these are the names of the mutual funds. Each fund is managed by a portfolio manager and is designed to meet a certain goal, like giving the investor income through dividends, or like buying new companies that the manager thinks will grow and make a lot of money for investors.

NAV: The net asset value, or what a share of the fund is worth and, consequently, what an investor has to pay for a share of the mutual fund. The NAV is also what an investor gets when he sells a share of the fund.

Dly % Ret.: The daily percent return, or the amount the fund gained or lost in value from the NAV on the day before. The number will always have a plus (+) or minus (−) sign in front of it just as it does in the stock tables. (The percent change is calculated by subtracting the price you see in the newspaper from the price listed the day before and then dividing that number by the price listed the day before.) The table makes it really easy because it just gives you the percent change. You don't have to do the math yourself each time.

YTD % Ret.: The year-to-date percent return, or the amount the fund has gained or lost since the beginning of the year. This number also will have a (+) or (–) sign in front of it and is calculated the same way as the daily percent return.

This is the mutual fund information you'll see most days when you check a financial publication or check for the mutual fund quotations online. Sometimes, at least once every three months starting on January 1, the funds provide investors with extra information called the Mutual Funds Quarterly Review. You can see this example below.

Quarterly Mutual Funds Listing

A

GO TO: B|C|D|E|F|G|H|I|J|K|L|M|N|O|P|Q|R|S|T|U|V|W|Y

Friday, October 02, 2009

VIEW AS SPREADSHEET

Alphabetical listing by fund family. Three-year, five-year and 10-year returns are annualized. Rank compares performance among funds with same investment objectives for time periods listed. A=top 20%, B=next 20%, C=middle 20%, D=next 20%, E=bottom 20%.
See investment objective codes

Family/ Fund	Symbol	Inv obj	Assets (millions)	NAV	3rd Qtr	YTD	% TOTAL RETURN & RANK								Expense ratio
							1-year		3-year		5-year		10-year		
AARP Funds: (800-958-6457)															
Aggr p	AAGSX	BL	$28	9.34	14.2	20.1	1.1	C	-1.2	C	NS	..	NS	..	0.24
Consrv	AACNX	BL	22	10.15	7.5	10.9	8.5	A	4.2	A	NS	..	NS	..	0.25
Mod p	AAMDX	BL	47	9.84	10.8	15.6	5.2	B	1.7	A	NS	..	NS	..	0.24
Family/ Fund	**Symbol**	**Inv obj**	**Assets (millions)**	**NAV**	**3rd Qtr**	**YTD**	**1-year**		**3-year**		**5-year**		**10-year**		**Expense ratio**
AFBA 5Star Funds: (800-243-9865)															
Balancedl r	AFBAX	BL	$36	10.23	11.0	12.6	-2.7	E	0.9	B	4.8	A	6.0	A	1.07
LrgCpGrw I r	AFGLX	LG	30	10.26	13.4	10.6	-15.1	E	-6.3	E	-0.7	E	1.2	A	1.28
SmCapA t	AFCAX	SC	9	9.48	17.0	28.3	-2.0	B	-6.6	D	-0.2	E	NS	..	1.53
SmCapC t	AFCCX	SC	3	8.79	16.9	27.6	-2.7	B	-7.2	D	-0.9	E	NS	..	2.28
Family/ Fund	**Symbol**	**Inv obj**	**Assets (millions)**	**NAV**	**3rd Qtr**	**YTD**	**1-year**		**3-year**		**5-year**		**10-year**		**Expense ratio**
AIM Funds A: (800-959-4246)															

Source: Wall Street Journal

As you can see, some of the stuff we already talked about is in there. But there are some new columns, and they have very good information in them. There's one long heading called "% Total Return & Rank" (sometimes this is called "Performance & Rank," but it means the same thing). Under the "% Total Return & Rank" heading are several columns with headings of their own. That's where the real clues are lurking. These columns tell you how much the fund gained (+) or lost (–) over a set period of time. The figures under the subheadings include all of the dividends you might have earned if you owned the fund for one, three, or five years and left your dividends to be reinvested. This is a lot like the power of compounding—you make more money on the money you already made.

You will also see a letter after the one-, three-, and five-year total return. (Sometimes a ten-year figure is included too.) These letters are just like grades. They tell you how the fund compares to other funds of the same type. So, for example, if you see that a growth fund has an "A" in the ranking column, you know that it ranked in the top 20% of all growth funds in total return. If it has a "B" it's in the next 20% down, and so on—until you get to the fateful "E," which means the fund ranked with the worst funds for total return. If a fund has several Es, then you should stay away from it—but you probably figured that out already.

Sometimes these columns don't include numbers for a particular mutual fund; instead they have the abbreviation "NS." This means that the fund did not exist during that time period. If there is an NS, it's usually under the five-year heading, but sometimes the fund is only one or two years old, so you see the abbreviation in several of the columns.

Here are the meanings of the other columns:

Objective (Inv obj): This term refers to the types of stocks the fund usually buys. There are thousands of mutual funds, but each of those funds is supposed to fit under a specific category. There are gold funds that invest in gold mines and gold coins; there are Pacific Region funds that invest only in stocks of Japan, China, and other Asian countries; there are European funds that only buy stocks from Germany, France, and other European countries; there are health and biotechnology funds that invest only in companies that make medicine and other health-related things. That's just the beginning. Each type of fund has two letters that identify the category it belongs to: "AU" for gold, "PR" for Pacific Region, "EU" for Europe, and "HB" for health and bio-technology. Two of the biggest selling categories are growth funds ("GR"), which invest in smaller companies that look like they might grow bigger and get richer, and growth-and-income funds ("GI"), which invest in some companies that are expected to grow bigger and in other companies that already give steady dividends or income. When these quarterly reviews appear in the paper, a list of the meanings of these abbreviations is included.

Max Sales Charge: This is the maximum charge for placing an order. When brokers sell certain mutual funds, they get commissions, just as they do when they sell stocks. With mutual funds, it is called a *sales charge* or *load*, and the load comes out of what you paid for your shares of the fund. Many funds charge a maximum initial charge so they can pay the broker who sold it to you "up front" (which means the minute you buy the fund). This is called an *up-front* or *front-end load*. You can compare the fees of different funds by comparing this number down the column with the heading "Initial." If zeros appear in this column, that means there is no initial charge or up-front load. The funds with zeros are called *no-load funds*. Sometimes a fund that does not charge an up-front load will make investors pay when they sell their fund shares. That figure is under the column with the heading "Exit." When you are charged at the time you sell your shares, it's called a *back-end load*. The funds that charge back-end loads sometimes have a small "r" after the fund name. Just as for stock tables, newspapers usually include a chart that reminds you what the mutual fund table columns mean. Each paper does its own version, but they all guide you in the same way.

OK, that's it. As you can see, checking mutual fund tables is not so terribly different from looking at stock histories. It's actually a little bit easier, since you have the report card rankings to give you a quick clue. Now it's time to put what you've learned to work.

$ Read the Mutual Fund Tables

Look on the Vanguard Funds listings in the table on the next page and find a fund that ranks in the "A" category. Then find a fund than ranks in the "E" category. Has either improved or declined in performance over time? Now see if you can find the funds that are classified as growth funds and those that are growth-and-income funds. Next,

VANGUARD FDS   800-662-7447

Fund	Code	Min	Assets			Exp	NAV					
Intmdt-Tm Treas	IG	50K	1333	NO	NO	0.15	10.21	3.1	8.1	7.2A	6.0A	6.2A
Long-Tm Treas	LU	50K	442	NO	NO	0.15	10.62	2.8	11.8	9.5A	7.1A	7.1A
Sh Tm Treas	SU	50K	1048	NO	NO	0.15	9.97	2.5	5.7	6.1A	5.6A	5.8B
Asset Alloc	MP	3K	9045	NO	NO	0.49	24.79	1.1	6.2	11.4C	13.8A	17.0A
CA Ins Int Tx-Ex	IM	3K	1599	NO	NO	0.17	10.77	2.5	7.5	7.0A	5.0A	5.8A
CA Ins Lg Tx-Ex	NM	3K	1660	NO	NO	0.18	11.26	3.1	9.7	8.6A	5.2A	6.5A
Cap Oppty	XG	3K	5984	NO	NO	0.75	31.52	r0.8	31.2	80.6A	43.9A	28.3B
Convertible	MP	3K	373	NO	NO	0.55	14.98	2.5	14.4	37.9A	13.8A	15.1B
Energy	NR	3K	1243	NO	NO	0.48	28.41	r8.5	29.8	27.3C	5.0B	16.0B
Equity Income	EI	3K	2395	NO	NO	0.41	24.06	7.4	5.8	6.3D	9.4B	15.8A
Explorer Fund	SG	3K	4807	NO	NO	0.74	80.04	1.7	16.6	51.6C	16.1D	17.2C
FL Ins L-T Tx-Ex	NM	3K	888	NO	NO	0.18	10.94	2.3	7.3	7.0A	4.5A	5.9A
Glbl Ast All	MP	3K	112	NO	NO	0.58	11.02	r-0.3	2.9	7.7D	9.8C	10.8D
Glbl Equity	GL	3K	149	NO	NO	0.68	13.66	r-3.0	-3.4	6.8E	7.6D	11.0D
GNMA	MT	3K	13031	NO	NO	0.27	10.06	3.2	7.4	7.6A	5.9A	6.7A
Gold	AU	3K	321	NO	NO	0.77	6.98	r2.5	-16.8	-18.6A	-9.8A	-9.5A
Growth & Income	LV	3K	10146	NO	NO	0.37	35.71	1.6	-0.4	16.2A	16.5A	22.1A
Growth Equity	LG	10K	849	NO	NO	0.92	18.68	-1.2	8.2	51.1A	32.2A	30.4A
Health Care	HB	3K	15309	NO	NO	0.41	130.90	r9.5	46.0	59.7D	30.5B	30.6A
Hi Yld Corp	HC	3K	5630	NO	NO	0.29	7.04	r1.4	1.8	4.5A	4.2A	7.0A
Inflation-Protect Se	LU	3K	75	NO	NO	NA	10.15	2.1	NS	NS	NS	NS
Intl Gro	IL	3K	10144	NO	NO	0.58	20.79	-9.9	-7.6	12.6B	7.3C	10.7C
International Value	IL	3K	919	NO	NO	0.59	26.16	-9.6	-9.4	-2.6E	4.7D	7.4E
Intmdt Corp	IB	3K	1703	NO	NO	0.27	9.29	3.7	6.4	6.8A	5.2C	6.0B
Intmdt Treas	IG	3K	1639	NO	NO	0.27	10.44	3.2	8.1	7.1A	5.9A	6.1A
Lifestrategy Consv G	BL	3K	1794	NO	NO	NA	15.15	1.3	4.0	10.1C	10.0B	11.9C
Lifestrategy Growth	BL	3K	3740	NO	NO	NA	21.12	-0.5	0.2	13.1B	12.9A	16.1A
Lifestrategy Income	BL	3K	567	NO	NO	NA	13.04	2.4	6.3	8.6D	8.4C	9.7E
Star Moderate Gro	BL	3K	3818	NO	NO	NA	18.21	0.4	2.3	11.6C	11.5B	14.0B
Lg-Tm Corp	AB	3K	3611	NO	NO	0.30	8.19	3.4	6.5	5.6C	4.5C	6.0B
Lg-Tm Treas	LU	3K	1213	NO	NO	0.27	10.32	2.7	11.7	9.4A	6.9A	7.0A
MA Tax-Ex	SS	3K	162	NO	NO	0.20	9.47	2.7	7.8	6.7A	NS	NS
Morgan Growth	XG	3K	6187	NO	NO	0.43	22.55	-1.7	1.4	24.8E	18.4D	22.3D
Muni High Yield Tx-E	GM	3K	3007	NO	NO	0.18	10.27	2.7	6.8	5.4B	4.1A	5.6A
Muni Ins Lg-Tm Tx-Ex	NM	3K	2295	NO	NO	0.19	12.04	2.3	7.7	7.0A	4.5A	5.7A
Muni Intmdt-Tm Tx-Ex	IM	3K	8450	NO	NO	0.18	12.99	2.1	5.6	5.6A	4.3A	5.0B
Muni Long-Tm Tx-Ex	GM	3K	1628	NO	NO	0.18	10.64	2.3	7.5	6.7A	4.2A	5.7A
Muni Limited-Tm Tx-E	SM	3K	2754	NO	NO	0.18	10.62	1.7	4.1	4.4A	4.0A	4.3A
Muni Short-Tm Tx-Ex	SM	3K	1980	NO	NO	0.18	15.49	1.2	3.3	4.0B	3.8B	3.9C
NJ Ins L-T Tx-Ex	SS	3K	1197	NO	NO	0.19	11.40	2.5	7.2	6.5A	4.5A	5.5A
NY Ins L-T Tx-Ex	NM	3K	1590	NO	NO	0.20	10.68	2.3	8.0	7.1A	4.5A	5.6A
OH Ins L-T Tx-Ex	SS	3K	396	NO	NO	0.19	11.38	2.2	7.1	6.5A	4.3A	5.5A
PA Ins L-T Tx-Ex	SS	3K	1893	NO	NO	0.19	10.83	2.1	7.1	6.5A	4.4A	5.5A
Preferred Stk	MP	3K	209	NO	NO	0.36	8.75	2.8	1.5	-2.2E	1.8E	5.2E
Primecap	XC	3K	25071	NO	NO	0.51	68.75	-3.5	12.2	34.5A	23.4A	26.3A
REIT Index	SE	3K	1026	NO	NO	0.33	11.45	r7.5	21.8	20.9C	-0.3D	NS
Select Value	MV	3K	153	NO	NO	0.73	11.04	10.9	11.1	11.5E	-3.8E	NS
Star	BL	1K	8093	NO	NO	NA	18.51	5.1	9.0	15.0B	10.0B	14.0B
Sht-Tm Corp	SB	3K	7014	NO	NO	0.27	10.57	2.8	5.5	6.6A	5.7A	6.0A
Sht-Tm Federal	SU	3K	1447	NO	NO	0.27	9.99	2.5	5.6	6.3A	5.5A	5.8A
Strategic Equity	MV	3K	747	NO	NO	0.46	17.97	r4.9	7.2	23.2C	6.6C	16.0B
Sht-Tm Treas	SU	3K	1169	NO	NO	0.27	10.10	2.3	5.5	5.9B	5.5B	5.6B
Tax Mgd Balanced	BL	10K	416	NO	NO	0.20	19.29	r0.6	4.0	15.5A	12.1A	13.5B
Tx Mgd Cap App	XG	10K	3045	NO	NO	0.19	35.03	r-0.5	2.5	25.8E	19.8D	22.6D
Tx Mgd G&I	LC	10K	2577	NO	NO	0.19	31.17	r-0.9	-1.4	13.4D	16.5C	21.7B
Tx Mgd Intl	IL	10K	197	NO	NO	NA	10.54	r-8.0	-11.9	3.4D	NS	NS
Tx Mgd SmCp	SC	10K	324	NO	NO	0.19	14.21	r4.8	12.7	26.8C	NS	NS
US Growth	LG	3K	22331	NO	NO	0.39	46.33	1.1	6.4	27.9C	23.8C	25.3B
US Value	XV	3K	60	NO	NO	NA	10.84	10.3	NS	NS	NS	NS
Utilities	UT	3K	864	NO	NO	0.40	16.04	13.6	17.5	18.0D	16.3D	14.7E
Wellesley Income	MP	3K	6202	NO	NO	0.31	19.76	6.9	9.3	8.3D	7.2D	10.4D
Wellington Income	BL	3K	22423	NO	NO	0.30	28.12	4.7	3.4	6.0D	7.6D	12.9C
Windsor	XV	3K	15918	NO	NO	0.28	16.07	7.8	6.8	13.2B	5.1D	13.1C
Windsor II	LV	3K	23606	NO	NO	0.37	27.11	10.5	9.8	7.8D	7.8D	16.0D

pick one of the funds in the chart. Fill in the middle row of boxes in the table below. Then look it up in a current financial publication or online. Fill in the bottom row of boxes. Has it improved or declined in performance over time?

	Fund Name	Fund Obj	One Year	Ranking Guide	Three Year	Ranking Guide
August 2000						
Today's Date						

	Fund Name (continued)	Five Year	Ranking Guide	Ten Year (if available)	Ranking Guide	Max Initial Charge
August 2000						
Today's Date						

What are the key things you looked at to determine the fund's history? Place an X next to each category that helped you.

Fund Name _____

Objective _____

One-Year Return _____

Three-Year Return _____

Five-Year Return _____

Ten-Year Return _____

Max Sales Chrg _____

For an overview of how to make investment decisions about stocks and mutual funds, go to www.stockmarketinvestinginfo.com/smi_stocktypes .html or www.investopedia.com/university and take the tutorials.

Billy Ray Picks Some Funds

Billy Ray decided he wanted to divide his savings into thirds, each with a different risk level. He did some research about investments, but he wasn't quite sure what mix would be best.

Billy Ray went to school with a young woman whose father was a financial planner. He went to this financial planner, told him his plan, and asked for advice. Billy Ray thought about all the things his friend's dad told him and looked over all the information he gave him. Then Billy Ray made his decision.

At age 20 Billy Ray bought three mutual funds. For his high-risk fund he picked the Alliance Technology Fund, Class B, which is managed by the Alliance Capital Group. For his medium-risk fund he chose the MFS Emerging Growth Fund, managed by MFS Investment Management. For his low-risk investment he bought shares in the Washington Mutual Investors Fund, managed by the American Funds Group. Each of these funds has a management style that fit his goals. Also, the Washington Mutual Investors Fund has no alcohol or tobacco stocks in it, and this appealed to him.

He plans to stay with these funds for the long run. In his words, "I'm in for the duration." He adds to these three funds when he can, and then he sits back and lets them earn money for him. But Billy Ray doesn't stop here.

In this chapter you learned all about how to read the clues to pick your investments wisely. You learned

- where stock tables are published,
- how to understand the stock table abbreviations,
- how to interpret stock table numbers,
- where mutual fund tables are published,

- how to understand mutual fund table abbreviations,
- and how to interpret mutual fund numbers.

Now you know the basic information needed to look at stock and mutual fund tables. You have all the tools in place to play the investment game. At this moment, you understand enough to walk into a brokerage office and place an order for stocks, bonds, or mutual funds, or you could do it over the phone or online. Yet with investments, just like sports, there are some big-picture issues you need to know before you become a highly skilled player. You need to learn some of the signs that tell you if the stock market is getting tired or if workers are spending more than they did two years ago. You need to know how and why the U.S. government tries to fix things. All of these issues have to do with the bigger economic picture, which is covered in the next chapter.

All About the Economy

WHY NIKES COST MORE WHEN IT FLOODS IN CHINA

Economics

To MANY PEOPLE, especially adults, *economy* and *economics* are scary words. Adults hear these words all the time on the news or see them in newspapers or magazines, but they don't know what they mean. These words don't have to be scary. They're very simple, especially when the economy is broken down into its various parts.

A famous economist named Alfred Marshall once said that economics is "the study of mankind in the ordinary business of life." That's really what it is. It's the study of life with a special interest in saving and spending. It's the study of money and how it circulates. It's the study of people and their saving patterns. It's the study of investing trends. It's the study of how people's minds work and what makes them save or not save. Economists study why people buy certain stocks or bonds and then what causes them to sell them. And they study what things cost—yesterday, today, and what they might cost tomorrow. The best part of all this is that you already know a lot about most of these things by now, so you need not be afraid.

Macroeconomics and Microeconomics

Before we get started, there are a couple of new terms you should know. These are *macroeconomics* and *microeconomics*. They are both big and pretty impressive words, and each sounds good when you say it. Think of Big Macs when you say macroeconomics because, in a way, the subject matter is like a Big Mac—it has it all. Macroeconomists know how many people work in the whole country and how many can't find jobs. They even know how many people are employed in your state and how many are jobless in your town. They look at how many houses are built each month, and they find out how many are built in states around the country, like California, Illinois, or Florida. They even look at weather patterns and know when it floods in China. (They know how the floods in China cause your Nikes to cost more, because your Nikes are made in China.) Macroeconomists study big things. The study of the details is left to microeconomists.

Microeconomics is not about the big picture; it's about all the little pieces that make up the big picture. It's about companies that make things and stores that sell things. It's about how companies that make similar products compare with each other, such as Nike and Reebok or the Gap and J. Crew or Coca-Cola and Pepsi. It's about yearly sales for each of these companies and how much they spend on television ads during the

Super Bowl and how much they earned per share of stock. Finally, it's about whether a particular company does better or worse than the other companies that sell the same products.

To sum up, macroeconomics is like seeing your city or town from one of those blimps that you sometimes can see floating over ballparks and football stadiums. From this view you can see the bigger shapes of things like highways, schools, and churches. You can count the number of schools by the number of playgrounds or playing fields you see, or you can count the number of churches by counting the number of steeples or domes. But you can't see any details. You can't even find your own house. In contrast, microeconomics is like moving through your city or town on a skateboard. You can skate past a school or a church and then over to the shopping mall nearest your house. You can see that there are a lot of cars in the parking lot and you can even count the number of people going into the Gap. But you can't tell how many people are in J. Crew in the mall on the other side of town unless you skate over there and count. Only when you compare the two stores can you tell which one is more successful.

$ Follow the Weather

Listen to the national news on TV or on the radio. If you have cable TV, turn on the Weather Channel. You can also go online and visit www.weather.com. See if there is a mention of a major weather event somewhere in America, like a thunderstorm, snowstorm, tornado, or flood. Then see if the program or Web site article talks about businesses being closed or people unable to work because of the weather. Think about what these events have to do with the economy. If a lot of households are damaged, who will pay for the repairs? Will homeowners have to take money from their savings accounts? Who will rebuild the homes? Will local carpenters and electricians have more work than they can handle? Will they have to hire more workers? Do you remember Hurricane Katrina and how it closed down the economy of New Orleans? Think of all the people from around the country who were hired to help put the city back together again.

Next, listen to your local news or read your local newspaper. Find a story that shows people affected by the weather. Have basements flooded? Have cars stalled in the deep water? Think about what that might mean for the economy of your town. Will your neighbors have to buy new basement furniture? Will they buy the furniture from the store in town? Will the storeowner then have a lot more money to buy more furniture for his store?

The Economic Checkup

Let's start with the big picture, the macroeconomic picture. Remember that economics is about life. It's about jobs, savings, investing, and money. It's also about floods, hurricanes, and tornadoes; the damage they cause; and who pays for that damage. Macroeconomists measure the economic health of our country. They're like family doctors—they decide if the country is sick, and then they decide on a cure.

How do economists measure our country's economic health? They do it just as your doctor does at your annual checkup. Your doctor weighs you, measures your height, feels your pulse, listens to your chest, looks in your ears, and makes you say "ah" when she puts that awful tongue depressor way back in your throat. By checking all of these things, she can tell if you are healthy. The only difference between a physical checkup by a doctor and an economic checkup by macroeconomists is that they check different things. Here are the major questions macroeconomists ask when they check America's economic health:

- How many Americans want to work but can't find jobs?

- How many new houses are being started each month?

- How many back orders do factories have? (Here they're interested in factories that produce big-ticket items, such as machinery, tractors, or cars.)

- How many new orders are being placed at factories that make consumer goods, such as shoes, clothes, video games, and cell phones?

- How much money is in circulation? (Remember that money circulates from person to person as people buy and sell things and pay bills. Economists look at this money circle for all consumers in the country.)

The economy is like a giant jigsaw puzzle, and the answer to each of the checkup questions is a puzzle piece. As economists examine one piece after another and fit it into its place, the puzzle picture becomes clearer. Finally, when enough pieces have been filled in, the picture comes together. By looking at each piece in connection to the others, economists can tell if the economy is healthy or sick. They also can do something about it if they see an economic "cold" coming on.

Economic Clues

Here are the clues economists get from key economy puzzle pieces:

Jobless claims: Jobless claims show how many people are out of work. The official phrase is "unemployment figures." If unemployment figures go down, it means that more people are working. When people work, they spend the money they make. If more people are working, then there is more money in circulation and the economy grows.

Housing starts: Housing starts, or the construction of new houses, give economists another clue about economic health. When people buy new houses, it means they feel good about their jobs and the amount of money they have to spend. It also means that the economy is strong and there is more money in circulation. If housing starts are down, it means just the opposite. It means that people are not so confident about their jobs, and they don't want to spend their money—especially not on something as expensive as a house.

Durable goods: Economists check on back orders for big manufactured products, like cars, planes, and tractors. These large, heavy products that last a long time are called *durable goods*. Economists check to see how many orders have been placed for durable goods and then they count how many orders have not been filled. The ones that are not filled are called *back orders*. The number of back orders gives economists a clue about how confident companies are about their sales. For instance, if a lot of people want to buy cars, car dealers will place such big orders that car manufacturers can't keep up with them. That's a good sign for the economy, even though it might be bad for the buyer who wanted to drive off the lot instantly in a new car.

Consumer goods: Economists also check new factory orders for consumer goods. *Consumer goods* are things that we use up, like shoes, cereal, and toothpaste. Consumer goods have to be replaced fairly often, since we grow out of our shoes, eat up all our cereal, and use the toothpaste until no more can be squeezed out of the tube. When people buy a lot of consumer goods, it means two things: First, it means there's a lot of money in circulation. Second, it means people feel good about the economy.

Leading economic indicators: There's a quick way to do an economic checkup, just as a blood test can check for a lot of things at one time. It's called the Index of Leading Economic Indicators, often shortened to "leading indicators" or "the Index." The leading indicators make up a kind of monthly economic report card. Ten indicators, including the questions we've already looked at, make up the Index. Each indicator is assigned a point value—its "grade"—depending on its strength of activity. When the points are all added up, the economy gets a score for the month. Economists learn a lot about America's economic growth based on whether the leading indicator score goes up or down from month to month. When it goes up three months in a row, it's a sign that the economy is growing. If it goes down three months in a row, economists start to worry that the economy is getting sick. Investors can tell the same things.

$ Check the Health of the Economy

Look in the business section of a newspaper or search online for leading economic indicators. Look for graphs or discussions of the four indicators discussed above: jobless claims, housing starts, durable goods, and new factory orders. Are housing starts going up or down? What does that mean? Now look at the other indicators. What are the most recent unemployment figures? When thinking of all these indicators together, how would you say the economy is doing?

Now look for a leading indicators graph. Are the indicators going up or down? What does that mean for investors? Sit down and talk to someone about your views. Explain why you think the economy is healthy or getting sick. You may even decide to use what you've learned for a class at school. Remember, if you can write it or say it, it means you know it.

The Health of the Economy and the Doctor, the Federal Reserve System

One of the best ways to measure the economic health of the country is to measure the money supply. *Money supply* means the cash people have at their fingertips to spend on things. It's measured by the amount of money families have in bank accounts and the investments they have in funds that can be sold immediately. The leading indicators that were discussed above provide a pretty clear picture of the economy puzzle. When economists discover the money-supply piece, the jigsaw puzzle is complete.

There is something very special about the money supply. Not only does the money supply help economists measure the country's economic health, but it can also be used as medicine if the economy shows signs of getting sick. A special group of economists does this. They work for the Federal Reserve System and serve on the Board of Governors of the Federal Reserve, which is usually referred to as "the Fed." The Fed can regulate the money supply, which makes it very powerful. In fact, economists and investors eagerly watch the Fed's every move.

In many families, one person is in charge of paying bills and balancing the checkbook. In the United States it's the same way, but instead of one person, our country has a group of seven people who keep track of the nation's checkbook. The Fed members are appointed by the president of the United States and, if approved by Congress, they serve a 14-year term. This means they become very familiar with the health of the economy, just as your family doctor is very familiar with your health.

The seven Fed members, along with a special committee called the Open Market Committee, are the people who keep a constant watch on the money supply in our country. They are the doctors who dole out the medicine to keep the economy healthy.

A Giant Allowance

The money supply is like a giant allowance, and the country does exactly what you do when you get your allowance. It spends most and sometimes saves some. The key is this: If people in America have more money to spend, they spend it. If they have less, they don't spend it. By controlling the money supply, the Fed controls how much Americans spend. (I'll explain how they do this next.) It all has to do with the amount of money in circulation.

Remember that the Fed carefully watches the leading indicators. By doing these regular economic checkups, the Fed can tell if the economy is getting a little hyperactive or if it's getting slow and sluggish. They call the hyperactivity "inflation." When the economy is suffering from inflation, prices go up. This is because people have more cash to spend.

Do you remember that when a lot of people want to buy the same stock, the seller can charge more? Well, it's the same with most things we buy. Say your mom or dad gets a raise in September and your family has more money to spend for the holidays than usual. But a lot of other people received raises too. Everyone feels confident so they all decide to buy more holiday gifts, including smart phones. Apple bets its newest iPhone is going to be a big seller. Since there is a limited supply of iPhones and a lot of people who have extra money, Apple figures customers will pay a lot to get one. So the company puts a higher price on the new version than on the older models. In other words, Apple inflates the price of the newest iPhone.

If the price of one product goes up, especially one that you can live without, that's OK; but if the prices of real necessities, like food, gasoline, and medicine, all go up, that's bad news. It means that the value of a dollar has gone down, because you can't buy as much as you used to with that dollar. If inflation gets out of hand, the economy doesn't work as well as it should. Because of this, the Fed keeps a close eye on the prices companies charge consumers for their products.

The opposite of an inflationary economy is a sluggish economy. When the economy is sluggish, economists are afraid it might go into what is called a *recession*. In a recession the economy is incredibly sluggish, hardly able to move. A recession happened in America and in other parts of the world in 2008 and 2009. The Fed saw it coming because they were watching the leading economic indicators. They saw that a lot of people were unemployed, housing starts were down, and there were only a few back orders for cars and trucks. To the Fed that meant our country was in big trouble and the trouble could get even worse if they didn't take action. (I'll tell you what they did before long. It's a good story.) The key thing was that Americans had begun to feel poor. And when people feel poor, they are scared to buy anything extra. They lose confidence in the economic well-being of the country.

Consumer Confidence (Even the Country Can Have an Attitude)

The economy has moods, or at least shoppers have moods. When we're in a good mood and we feel comfortable about money, we tend to do things like go out to movies and get hot fudge sundaes on the way home. We may even stop at a bookstore and buy a couple of new books. When we're in a good mood, we tend to spend money. When we're in a bad mood, though, we don't like to go out at all. We stay home and mope, and we tend to hang on to every penny because we're afraid that it is the last penny we will ever earn.

Economists have a term for our moods. It's called *consumer confidence*. *Consumer* means someone who buys things. Since all of us buy things, we are all consumers. High consumer confidence means that we feel good about our current and future money supply, like when it's early summer and you know you'll have a lot of yard jobs and make a lot of money before it gets cold. Low consumer confidence means just the opposite.

Economists spend a lot of time tracking consumer confidence for a couple of reasons. Consumer confidence reflects the health of the economy—its strength or weakness. At the same time, consumer confidence can change the health of the economy. Let's say that the economy is healthy; that is, unemployment is low and people are buying cars. But consumers don't feel good about the future. Some people are afraid the plant where they work is going to close; others are upset because houses cost more than they can afford. So they mope around—they don't go out and they don't spend much money. When a lot of consumers start to mope around, the economy starts to mope around too. It gets sluggish. Sometimes the Fed even has to step in and put us on a diet called an easy-money policy (explained on page 86), so that the economy won't get really sick.

Consumer confidence can help heal the economy too. Let's say this time that the economy is sluggish for several months, but it's been a good growing season for farmers because there was a lot of rain after the crops were planted. Also two new car plants are being built in North Carolina that will provide hundreds of new jobs. Americans are happy and employed, so they're not afraid of the future. Because they're not afraid, they begin to spend money. As consumer money begins to flow back into the economy, the economy starts to speed up and, before long, it's healthy again.

These patterns are called *economic cycles*. The word *cycle* comes from a Greek word that means *circle* or *wheel*. The economy goes around and around, and consumer confidence does the same thing. Sometimes it's low, then it gets high, and then it gets low again; and sometimes consumer confidence drives the economic wheel.

Check Inflation

Do an inflation check. Try to remember how much you or your folks paid for new shoes or a winter coat last year. If you can't remember, ask the family member or friend who helped you pick out the item if he or she remembers. Then go to the mall and check the price for the same shoes or coat. Did the price stay the same, or does the item cost more this year? You might check other things you bought last year, such as downloaded music or video games.

What about gas prices? Is gas more or less expensive this year than last year? What about food prices? If you don't usually help with the shopping, ask someone who does. What about the price of milk, cereal, and peanut butter? Copy the table on the next page to keep track of your comparisons. When you compare the figures, you will get a clear idea of whether or not we're in a period of inflation.

Inflation Check

	This Year's Price	Last Year's Price
Shoes		
Winter Coat		
Sweatshirt		
Music Downloads		
Video Game		
Big Mac		
Milk		
Cereal		
Gasoline		
Anything Else You Want to Compare		

If you want to get fancy, you can express the inflation increase or decrease as a percentage. If prices have gone up, subtract last year's price from this year's, and then divide the difference by last year's price. Move the decimal point two places to the right. The number you get is the percentage increase in inflation for one year. For example, if sweatshirts sold for $18 last year but for $20 this year, the inflation increase is 11% (20 − 18 = 2; 2 ÷ 18 = .11 or 11%). If prices have gone down, subtract this year's price from last year's price, and then divide the difference by last year's price. Move the decimal point two places to the right. The number you get is the percentage decrease in inflation for one year.

If you completed this part of the activity, then you just did what economists do every day. Congratulations!

Regulating the Money Supply

Based on the diagnosis of inflation or recession, the Fed will prescribe one of two things: it will either put us on a tough diet, called a *tight-money policy*, to help control inflation, or it will put us on a pretty good diet, called an *easy-money policy*, to help a sluggish economy avoid a recession. Another way to say it is that the Fed decreases or increases the country's allowance.

When the Fed enacts a tight- or an easy-money policy, it is regulating the money supply. The Fed can regulate the money supply in a number of ways, but the most common way is for the Fed to buy or sell government securities. (Remember those treasury notes and bonds from chapter 3?) The Fed buys or sells treasuries the same way we make our trades in stocks or bonds. The only difference is that the Fed does it every day. Each day shortly after 11 A.M., the Federal Reserve Bank of New York either buys or sells treasury securities. If the Fed thinks there is too much money floating around out there, it can decide to take some of it back by selling treasuries. Banks or brokerage houses buy treasuries because they have customers who would like to invest in them. When banks buy them, it uses up some of their cash and they can't lend it to people for cars, homes, or college educations. Therefore the money supply is tightened and the Fed is following a tight-money policy. On the other hand, if the Fed thinks the economy is getting sluggish—people are not spending money—then it buys some treasuries. When the Fed buys treasuries from banks or brokerage houses, all that cash the Fed paid for them is put back into circulation, which makes it easier for people to borrow money from banks for expensive things. When this happens the Fed is following an easy-money policy.

The other way that the Fed regulates the money supply is to change the discount rate. The *discount rate* is the interest rate the Fed charges local banks to borrow money from it. If the Fed decides the economy is growing too quickly and fears that prices will rise too high, it tries to slow that down. It makes banks pay more to borrow money; that is, it increases the discount rate. If the Fed thinks the economy is getting sluggish because consumer spending is down, it tries to stimulate spending. It charges banks a lower rate to borrow money; that is, it lowers the discount rate.

When the Fed acts to increase or decrease the discount rate, it's like hitting the first domino in a domino line. When banks have to pay more to borrow money, they usually decide they don't want to borrow as much—or they may even decide not borrow any at all. This means that they have less money to lend out and are charging higher rates for the money they do loan, which cuts down the money supply. On the other hand, if the Fed charges banks less to borrow money, banks may decide to borrow as much as they can. This means there's more money circulating and it's easier to borrow. It's the allowance thing again—the Fed either decreases or increases the country's allowance.

During the 2008–2009 recession, the Fed moved into an easy-money policy. It had been watching unemployment rise and house purchases drop. Plus only a few people were buying big-ticket items like cars and boats. Some people could not even pay their mortgages each month and were about to lose their homes. So the Fed stepped in. It dropped the discount rate so that banks could borrow more money and lend it out to people for cars and houses. It even gave banks big chunks of money to lend to new businesses to help those businesses get started. That's how worried the Fed was about a recession. It gave money to car dealers to give to their customers through the Car Allowance Rebate System, also known as Cash for Clunkers. That program encouraged people to turn in their old cars for cars that got good gas mileage—a two-for-one deal because it also helped improve carbon emission levels to help with pollution. Plus the Fed distributed money to states and local governments to upgrade roads and bridges, which in turn led to more jobs for construction workers and suppliers. Because of all these actions (and some additional regulations to keep a sluggish economy from turning into nearly dead economy), the recession turned a corner in late 2009.

The Fed is able to make money regulation policies because it runs America's national bank. I should really say *banks*, because there's not just one big bank in the United States—there are 12 big banks. These 12 banks are called *district banks*, and they are spread throughout the country. Each part of the country has its own Fed-run bank. In addition to these 12 banks, there are 25 midsize banks called *regional* or *branch banks*, also found all over the country. The key thing to remember is that the banks that make up the Federal Reserve System are the biggest banks in the country, and when a smaller bank runs a little low on cash, it turns to a Fed bank for a loan.

The Fed Is More than a Doctor

The Fed does a lot more than regulate the nation's money supply. As I just mentioned, the Fed is in charge of the district and regional banks that make up America's national banking system. These are the banks that take old money out of circulation and issue new money (which we talked about in chapter 1).

The Fed also serves as a safe-deposit box for foreign governments. Foreign countries store gold in the Federal Reserve Bank of New York to use when money changes hands between countries. It is stored in a huge vault that holds approximately 10,000 tons of gold. That's a lot of gold—in fact, it's estimated to be the most gold kept in one place anywhere in the world.

As for the national checkbook, the Fed also keeps track of bank accounts for the U.S. Department of the Treasury and other government offices. It writes more than 80 million treasury checks a year, including checks for your grandparents' retirement funds. Not only does it write the checks, it also has to keep a national check register. Can you imagine keeping track of 80 million checks? Not only does the Fed balance the checkbook, it also makes sure that the banks in the Federal Reserve System are following all the rules that the government has set to protect our money.

As if the Fed didn't have enough to do, it also is the national clearinghouse for checks. What this means is that every time you write a check or you or your parent receives a paycheck or someone pays a bill, the Fed helps those checks get to the right bank—and quickly. That's every check written by everybody every day. That totals more than 15 billion checks a year—that's 15,000,000,000! As you can see, the Federal Reserve, with all of these essential responsibilities, is very important to this country's economy.

Visit a Federal Reserve Bank

Wherever you live, try to visit a Federal Reserve district or regional bank. The 12 district banks are located in Boston, New York, Philadelphia, Richmond, Cleveland, Atlanta, Chicago, St. Louis, Minneapolis, Kansas City, Dallas, and San Francisco. If you live in New York City or anywhere nearby, visit the gold vaults at the Federal Reserve Bank of New York. They give guided tours, and you'll learn a lot.

You can find out the locations and tour information for the regional Fed banks by going to www.federalreserve.gov. From that site you can find out everything about the Fed system and the individual banks. You can get a quick overview of how the Fed works, watch a video about its history, and take the "Fed 101" course. There is an excellent glossary, plus you can check on current monetary policy. But be careful, because there are a lot of games you can play that make you lose track of time.

Find the Fed in the Media

Because the Fed is so central to this country's economy, you'll often see or hear the words "Federal Reserve Board" or "the Fed" in the media. See if you can find the Board of Governors of the Federal Reserve mentioned in the business section of a newspaper or in a magazine. What about leading economic indicators like housing starts or auto sales? Now turn on a TV or radio news program and listen to the business portion of the broadcast. Is the Fed mentioned or consumer confidence? If you have cable television, turn on a business channel and keep track of how many times the Fed or one of the leading indicators is mentioned in one 15-minute period.

Billy Ray Is Confident About the Economy

In 1998 Billy Ray was 21, playing basketball for the Georgetown College Tigers. He was still a star and still called "the Legend." His lawn-mowing business was going well, and he was putting his earnings into his mutual funds, but he was starting to think about investing his savings in another way. He wanted to buy some land.

He started looking around, and before long he found the parcel of land of his dreams: a 7.2-acre piece of farmland on the outskirts of Mount Sterling, Kentucky. The property had a pond on it, and he thought it would be great to build a house there some day. Billy Ray had a girlfriend and wanted to get married in a few years. But the farmland was more than a place to build a house; Billy Ray thought it would be a good investment.

Mount Sterling was growing and people were building houses on the outskirts of town. As more people wanted land, the land would increase in value (just as when a lot of people want to buy a stock that has a limited number of shares). Billy Ray was confident that Mount Sterling would continue to grow because there were new factories on the edge of town, three major universities each only 35 miles away, and several small colleges nearby. He thought that before long those 7.2 acres would be worth a lot more than the asking price, so he decided to buy the parcel.

He went to the bank again, but instead of asking for a small business loan, he applied for a mortgage. A *mortgage* is a type of loan that helps people buy a house or land. The bank makes the borrower pay part of the cost of the property up front and then lends him the money for the rest, with the understanding that he will pay the bank a certain interest rate to use its money for a specified period of time. Sometimes this time period can be as long as 30 years. (Remember from chapter 2 that one way the bank can pay you interest on your savings account is by letting other people borrow your money.) Mortgages are one of the most popular kinds of loans, because hardly anyone has enough money to pay the full price for a house or land at one time.

Because Billy Ray had been planning to look for land since the previous winter, he had enough savings set aside to put 10% down on the property; therefore his mortgage was for 90% of the cost of the land. Billy Ray being Billy Ray, he started immediately to pay more on his monthly mortgage than he had to. The sooner he could pay off his mortgage, the sooner he wouldn't have to pay the bank to use its money. Before long, he nearly had his mortgage paid off. Plus his prediction was right—land was getting scarce around Mount Sterling, and his land had increased in value in just one year. So even as Billy Ray was paying down his mortgage, his land was already worth more than he paid for it.

The days were beginning to get shorter, and winter—Billy Ray's thinking time—was on the way. Billy Ray started thinking about ways to make the best use of his land investment.

In this chapter you learned all about the economy. You learned about

- the terms *macroeconomics* and *microeconomics* and how economists use each one;
- the major clues to America's economy puzzle;
- the Federal Reserve System, its functions, and how central it is to this country's economy;
- the money supply;
- and the meaning and importance of consumer confidence.

You deserve to feel proud of all that you now understand—it's more than many adults know about how our economy works. To celebrate, go into the kitchen, pour yourself a big bowl of your favorite cereal, add a sliced banana, and pour on the milk. Then, as you eat, read the cereal box to discover what company produced it. You've just picked up a couple of potential stock investment tips. You'll find more suggestions on how to gather these tips and information in the next chapter.

All About Stock Picking

WHAT YOUR TOOTHPASTE TELLS YOU

Picking Stocks

NOW IT'S TIME to put it all together. You know about money and saving. You know about the miracle of compounding, and you know the difference between saving and investing. You know about Wall Street and about stock exchanges and about the Dow Jones Industrial Average. You know what to say when you want to place an order for stock or a mutual fund. You know how to read stock tables and how to compare stocks to see which one is the best buy. You know about the economy, the Fed, leading indicators, and consumer confidence. You know everything you need to know to be an investor—except for one thing. You still need to learn how to pick the right stock. That's what this chapter is all about. The tools for becoming a good stock picker are actually right at your fingertips.

Just Turn On the Lights

Stocks are divided into sectors, just as music is divided into genres. A stock's sector simply describes the type of company that is listed on a stock exchange. Instead of "rock," "R & B," or "country and western," stocks are listed under categories like "transportation," "financial," or "utilities." The names sound pretty boring when you compare them to music genres, but it's not so boring when you start making money from your utility or transportation investments.

One of the most popular stock sectors for the last century has been the utility sector. Utility companies provide us with gas for heating, electricity for lights and air conditioning, water for sprinkling the yard and flushing toilets, and telephone service for communicating with family and friends. When your family comes home late at night and your mom reaches around the corner to turn on the kitchen light, it may be Duke Energy (stock market abbreviation: DUK) providing the electricity for that light. When it's your turn to do the dishes, it may be American Water (AWK) that makes the soap bubble way up when you turn the water on full force or that fills the dishwasher (if you're lucky enough to have one). Utility companies provide us with these essentials.

One place to start learning about utility companies is in your own town. Ask an adult if you can look at the family's utility bills—the bills for water, electricity, gas, and telephone or Internet service. By looking at the bills you will see the name of the company that provides your family with these services. If you live in one of the South Atlantic states, Duke Energy may provide your power and CenturyLink (CTL) your phone service. If you live near Washington, D.C., it may be Washington Gas (WGL) that heats your furnace or provides you with gas to cook your food. No matter where you live in the United States, or even in the world, AT&T (T) might be your phone service provider. AT&T used to be the biggest phone company in the country. It still provides phone service for landlines, but now it's more interested in providing wireless Internet and cell phone service—two fast-growing markets.

All of the utility companies I've mentioned so far are considered good investments by a lot of people. That does not mean, though, that all utility companies are good buys. Utility companies are just like any other stock. You need to look into their histories and their financial data before you make an investment decision. You can use the Internet to research individual stocks—which you already know how to do.

A lot of investors purchase utility stocks for income because utility companies usually pay steady dividends. My mother and stepfather owned shares in a number of electric and gas companies. They were retired and wanted the income from their utility stocks coming in on a regular basis. Utilities are not just for older people, though. Utilities provide a stable base for anyone's investment portfolio. Since people will always need water, electricity, and phones, they're good investments, even for kids—especially since you don't have to take your dividends in cash. You can use them to buy more stock.

Dividend reinvestment plans, or DRIPs, allow investors to reinvest their dividends rather than take the dividends in cash. This means that approximately four times a year you'll get to buy a little more stock. You sign up for the DRIP plan with the company that issues your stock. When you buy the stock to begin with, the company may ask if you want to take your dividends or reinvest them. If the company doesn't ask the question, you should. Just say, "Do you offer dividend reinvestment plans?" If the person you are speaking to hesitates, say you are a beginning investor and that you would really rather own more stock than have the cash. If this kind of program is not already available, maybe you'll be able to talk the company into it.

Have You Looked at Your Toothpaste Lately?

Another interesting sector is called *consumer goods* or *consumer staples*. *Staples* are the products we use every day. Because we use them every day, we use them up and have to buy more. This means that the companies that make staple products are usually good investments.

You already know a lot of companies in this sector, but you just haven't thought of them in terms of investment possibilities. These potential investments include Coca-Cola (KO), Colgate-Palmolive (CL), Gillette (G), Johnson & Johnson (JNJ), Procter & Gamble (PG), and Sara Lee (SLE). I don't need to tell you what Coca-Cola makes, and I don't need to point out that Coca-Cola is something many families buy again and again. You probably already know that the Colgate-Palmolive Company makes toothpaste and toothbrushes. What you may not know is that Colgate-Palmolive also makes deodorant, bathroom and kitchen cleaner, laundry detergent, and diet pills. A lot of companies in the consumer staples sector make more things than people realize. The Sara Lee Corporation is a good example. If you've heard of Sara Lee, you probably know of it because of its sweet rolls, cookies, cakes, and pies. What you may not know is that Sara Lee also makes Ball Park Franks and sells coffee and tea.

The thing to remember about stocks in the consumer staple sector is that they are usually pretty stable. Although the value of a share may go up and down a little bit, you are not likely to lose all of your investment. That's because of the type of products these companies make—when people use up one of these products, they usually buy more.

Search for Consumer Staples

Go on a consumer staple sector search. Look in the linen closet and under the bathroom sink in your home. List the names of the companies that make the things you use every day. Sometimes you have to really look to find the name of the company, but it's always there somewhere on the packaging. Be sure to check the toothpaste, bath soap, razor blades, toilet paper, and cotton swabs.

Now look in the kitchen. Make a list of the companies that make the things under the sink. Check the dishwashing soap, surface cleaners, and paper towels. Next check the cupboards where your food is stored. Who makes the cereal, peanut butter, soup, and macaroni and cheese?

Finally, look in the financial section of the paper to see if you can find any of the company names on your list. Better yet, go online and research the company. Familiarize yourself with the company's products and its markets. Sara Lee, for example, sells in more than 40 countries. Jot down the company's symbol. Pick three companies to keep track of for the next three months.

Product	Manufacturer Symbol	Stock Price	Current Price	Month 1 Price	Month 2 Price	Month 3 Price

Computer Stocks

Every time you turn on the computer at home or in the classroom, you are touching a potential stock purchase. It may be the computer itself, made by Apple (APPL), Dell (DELL), or Hewlett-Packard (HPQ), or it may be the software that runs the computer, like Microsoft (MSFT) or Intel (INTC).

The stocks of companies that supply equipment for computers and other electronic devices are called *technology stocks* or just *technologies*. Technologies are big right now. (I probably didn't need to tell you that.) You may even be in class with someone who just designed a new app to make it easier to buy boomerangs from Australia from a smart phone.

Buying a technology stock is a lot different than buying a utility or a consumer staple stock. While the process is the same, the end result may be different because stocks of technology companies are riskier investments than stocks of utilities or consumer staples companies. This doesn't mean you shouldn't buy them. It just means you're taking a bigger chance with some technology stocks than you would with some other stock companies. Remember the investment formula: the higher the risk, the greater the potential return. So if your technology company turned out to be a good bet, you could make a lot more money than you would with a phone or cereal company.

Not all technology companies are high risk. IBM and Intel, which I named already, are pretty safe. There are others, such as Amazon.com (AMZN), that actually performed well during the 2008–2009 recession.

The Key

The key to all this stuff about stock picking is to simply look around you, then think, "What does my family buy over and over, and who makes it?" My grandchildren and I sometimes sit around the dinner table talking about how to choose a stock. When we have these conversations, someone always jumps up and checks who makes our favorite foods. One of my granddaughters eats a lot of macaroni and cheese—and I mean a *lot*. She should definitely invest in the stock of her favorite brand.

My grandchildren also poll their friends about what brands and items they like and the companies that make them. When you ask these kinds of questions, you're doing a consumer satisfaction survey. Companies pay a lot of money to marketing specialists for this kind of information. You can do your own survey just by researching and asking people questions. Asking other people what they think of a particular food brand, CD label, clothing line, store, or any other item or company is a great way to collect information, and this information will help inform your stock choices. If you do this, it's best to write it all down.

Here are some more ideas for you to research: What about the film industry? You already know about Disney (DIS), but what other companies produce films that draw long lines of people or that run in theaters for weeks and weeks? Don't forget about music. What CD labels produce the music you buy? Is there one company that shows up all the time? Check with friends to find out who they listen to and what labels their favorite artists are on. Who makes your favorite clothes? Check your own tags and ask your friends about their favorite clothes and who makes them. What stores do you shop at? Target (TGT) is big right now. Target stores are usually full of people, the service is good, the lines aren't too long, and you can return things without a hassle. Watch for those kind of things wherever you shop. Ask the adults in your family if they've ever shopped at Ethan Allen (ETH) for furniture or seen one of the company's catalogs. What about Bed Bath & Beyond (BBBY)? And don't forget the Home Depot (HD). The Home Depot is always jammed with people buying lumber, windows, light switches, kitchen cabinets, and more. Get an adult's opinion about the quality of the things these stores sell and whether these stores might be good investments.

Everywhere you look, if you really think about it, you will see a potential stock purchase. Then do your stock analysis homework and, if it looks like a good bet, jump in. Remember, not all of your stock purchases will be winners. If more than half are, you've truly learned about investing. In fact, even when you lose money on a stock or a mutual fund, you may still learn something. My grandfather used to say to me, "If you walk down the street with a fool and don't learn something, it might not be the fool's fault." It's true. You can learn just as much from bad choices as you can from good ones.

Conduct a Consumer Survey

Make a list of some of your favorite things, like clothes, musicians, and movies. You can also include some of your parents' favorite things and the stores where they like to shop. Write down the labels or brands of the objects you've listed. Keep track of the number of times you see someone using, wearing, or enjoying something on your brand list. The chart below will make it easy.

	COMPANY NAME, BRAND, LABEL, ETC.	NUMBER OF TIMES YOU SPOTTED THIS ITEM
Music		
Food		
Shoes		
Clothing		
Video Game		

What do your results tell you about the popularity of your choices? See if you can find the stock symbols for these companies. (All you have to do is do a search on the name of the company followed by "stock price.") Does the stock for any of these companies look like a good investment opportunity? Use what you learned in chapter 5 to make your decision.

Don't Forget About Mutual Funds

Stock mutual funds give you a way to buy shares in a number of stocks at one time and for less money than buying all those shares separately. (Refer to chapter 3 for the differences in buying shares of a stock and buying shares of a mutual fund.) Mutual funds come in all shapes and sizes. There are thousands to choose from. How do you pick the right ones?

Remember that Billy Ray decided that he wanted to split his investments into three parts—one-third for high-risk investments, one-third for medium risk, and one-third for low risk. Mutual funds make it easy for you to think in terms of risk because most are classified by investment goals. Instead of thinking in terms of stock sectors, like utilities or consumer staples, you make choices between investment needs, like current income or future growth. Under mutual fund investment goal headings, there are even further subheadings that define the goal. These headings include terms like *balanced* or *equity income, aggressive growth, small company growth*, and *global equity*. There are even sector funds that have only stocks of utility companies. The thing to remember is that these terms are descriptions that give the investor a general idea of the kinds of stocks in the funds.

Each of the management goals stated in a description of the fund relates to a certain level of risk. For example, Billy Ray's low-risk fund is an income fund in the Washington Mutual Investors Fund group of funds. The fund manager invests in stocks and bonds that give Billy Ray a steady return on his investment with little chance of losing his money.

Billy Ray's medium-risk fund is a growth-and-income fund called the MFS Emerging Growth Fund. Part of the fund is invested in stable securities that provide income, but there are also stocks that don't provide current income. Those stocks have a chance to increase in value and make money for the shareholders in the future.

Billy Ray's high-risk fund is a growth fund, Alliance Technology Fund, Class B, that invests in technology companies. Some are small companies that are just starting up and others are more established. With high-risk funds you take the chance your fund will lose value some years. You may even lose money on the fund if the portfolio managers gambled on some companies that just couldn't make it. But you also have the chance of increasing your investment like crazy, and it can feel really good to take that chance.

Check into Fund Families

Another way to pick mutual funds to fit your investment goal is to use a family of funds. Remember that a family of funds is a cozy way of saying that one mutual fund investment company has a lot of fund types available. It's a lot like Kellogg's, the company that makes cereal. Kellogg's doesn't just make one type of cereal—it makes Corn Flakes, Cheerios, Shredded Wheat, Rice Krispies, and granola. If you like one of its cereals, you could expect to like one of its others. Mutual fund families are the same. An investor says to herself, "I invested in Oak Associates White Oak Select Growth Fund and it did well. I think I'll see if Oak Associates has an aggressive growth fund." It does—the Pin Oak Aggressive Stock Fund. Plus Oak Associates also has funds that just invest in technology stocks and one that invests in health sciences. They would be worth checking out.

Mutual fund families make it easy for you to do your research. They provide information to potential customers on each of the funds they manage. They will even include the names of the stocks or bonds the manager has purchased to go in the fund. You can see how this works by going to www.oakfunds.com, where each of the Oak funds is listed with detailed information about the goal of the fund. Move around the site and look at names of the companies that the fund manager has picked to match the stated investment goal. You are now doing your research.

Find a list of fund families. Mutual fund families make it easy for you. They send you information that shows each of the funds they manage, and the goal of each fund. They will even include the names of some of the stocks each fund invests in.

Find Fund Families

If you are looking online, do a search for "mutual fund families." Explore some of the sites that come up. Bookstores are also a good place to look, as there are entire sections in the magazine section on finance and mutual funds. *Barron's* and *Money* magazines are good places to start. You will often find publications that list mutual funds by their levels of performance. If there are stars by the fund names, it means a research firm called Morningstar (www.morning star.com) has graded the fund (five stars are the best). Morningstar has a large and highly respected group of financial analysts; thus, stars from Morningstar are sought after by fund managers and potential investors.

Next, research a number of sites and publications. See if you can tell which companies offer the most fund choices to investors. After you've found a large family of funds, look under the heading marked "YTD % Ret" ("Year to Date % Return"). Compare the different returns. Look at the names of the funds. Can you tell anything about the stock types that are in the fund from the names? See if you can determine any connection between the names of the funds and the YTD % return. Now ask yourself, "If I were going to split my investment into three risk levels as Billy Ray did, does one of the fund families have a fund for each of my investment goals?" If it does and you have some money to invest, you've taken an enormous step toward becoming an investor.

Investing in Stocks or Mutual Funds

Which is the best investment—stock shares or mutual fund shares? How about investing in both? Mutual funds spread out your investments over a number of stock companies. By buying shares in a stock mutual fund, you protect your investment from total loss. On the other hand, the portfolio managers who manage your mutual fund investments do not work for free. You have to pay them part of what you earn on your investment each year to make stock choices for you. This is definitely something to take into account when you choose your investments. (Chapter 3 tells about the different fees for investing in mutual funds.)

When you purchase shares of stock directly from a broker or online, you pay a one-time fee to the broker who bought your stock for you through one of the exchanges. (Remember how the broker writes a ticket?) After that initial fee, there are no more costs. You don't have to pay a management fee year after year. You can pay yourself and invest what you pay yourself in more stock.

So the answer to the question of whether to invest in a mutual fund or stock is the following: consider investing in both. You will sleep at night knowing that a portfolio manager is watching over the stocks in your mutual fund, and you will smile to yourself during the day when you see that a stock you picked on your own just gained 9% in value. That gain is because something you thought might happen did! Plus there might be rumors of a merger where the stockholders will get two shares of the new company for each share in the old company. That's worth more than a smile; that's worth a laugh out loud and maybe a little dance step or two, especially since you know you figured it all out on your own.

Billy Ray Pays Himself

Billy Ray has a theory. It's that you pay yourself. Whenever he earns any money, he sets aside some to save and invest right away. He's done that since he was a kid shoveling snow in the winter or mowing lawns in the summer. He says it's like paying bills. Instead of paying for clothes or other things you want to buy, you first pay yourself. This money you pay yourself goes into your savings. So Billy Ray is paying himself and continues to plan his investments.

In the winter of 1999, Billy Ray was 22 and playing basketball for the Georgetown Tigers when he began to think about assets and equity. He had money in his savings account and in his mutual funds. Those savings and investments were his assets. He could continue to put money in his funds, which would increase his assets. But he wondered whether he should start to build up equity. He already had equity in his farmland. *Equity* is the difference between the value of land and the amount still owed on it. (Remember that Mount

Billy Ray

Sterling is growing and land values have increased.) Plus Billy Ray had been paying extra money on his mortgage. So he spent some dark winter evenings trying to decide the best place to put his money.

By the end of winter, Billy Ray decided to go for equity. He decided to use the money he made from his mowing company the next year to bring water, gas, and electricity to his land. He also decided to build a big garage with a small kitchen and bathroom, which he could live in for a year or so until he got married. He already had some equity in the land and a good record of making his mortgage payments. So he went back to the bank and asked to borrow some more money. He used the increased value of his farm to get a bigger mortgage, and then he got started. He put a road into the heart of the land. He built a water supply and a sewer system, which were things he would need for a house. Those two things cost the most. Then he brought in electricity so he could start to build his garage. He figured that after a couple of years his land would be worth even more, plus he had made all the improvements on his property, which further increased the value.

Billy Ray's goal was to build a large house on his land. He wanted to build up equity in the land and then go back to the bank to ask for a loan for the house. He hoped to have enough equity in his land in the future to get his mortgage without having to spend any of his savings.

Don't forget that all the time he was building equity, his mutual funds were still earning money for him and increasing his assets. Way to go, Billy Ray!

In this chapter you learned about picking stocks. You learned about

- stock sectors and stock abbreviations,
- dividend reinvestment plans,
- consumer surveys,
- and choosing between stocks and mutual funds or having some money in each.

The next chapter will help you ask some good questions and find some good answers along the investment trail.

All About
All of the Above

AND WHERE TO GO FOR MORE

Good Questions Usually Get Good Answers

When I was a graduate student at the University of Michigan, I sometimes felt my brain couldn't hold all the facts that I was learning. After a few years of more and more facts, I thought that any day I might start to forget what I learned at the beginning of my college career. Then I realized something that I have never forgotten: the sign of what you know about a subject is not the number of facts you can hold in your head. When you really understand a subject, it means you know the important questions to ask and where to find the answers.

I've thought of that realization a lot since I began writing this book. You don't need to remember all the facts I've included; you just need to understand enough to ask good questions. You also need to know where to get the best answers. These two tools will pave the road to your successful investment future. Remember that Billy Ray was never afraid to ask questions.

This chapter lists some questions and then gives some answers. A lot of the questions have to do with finding information: Where do I look for mutual fund information? Are there places to look for stock information online? Where do I find information for online brokers? Here we go!

Where do I find out savings rates at banks and credit unions?

- At www.e-wisdom.com, you can check out all sorts of things, including savings rates and certificate-of-deposit (CD) rates, plus credit card services and fees.

- For a list of banks and credit unions and their rates on all types of accounts, go to www.bankrate.com.

- For general information on credit unions, go to www.creditunions online.com.

Are there any banks that let kids have checking accounts?

I only know of one bank that is specifically for young investors. It's called the Young Americans Bank. Young Americans Bank will open checking and savings accounts for anyone age 12 and older. Young investors can even open a business checking account. If you live in the Denver area, classes are taught on money management and getting ahead in business. (If you are under 18, you have to have an adult cosign the checks.) A check card comes with your account, plus you can apply for a credit card. Young Americans Bank will open a savings account with as little as $10. You can also buy certificates of deposit. Finally, they send step-by-step directions for filling out a signature card. A signature card prevents anyone else from forging your name. It doesn't matter what state you live in;

you can mail in your checks or make withdrawals by mail. You can also check your accounts and transfer funds online through the bank's electronic banking service. By the way, they kick you out when you reach age 21. Here's the address and Web site:

Young Americans Bank
3550 East 1st Avenue
Denver, CO 80206
(303) 321-2265
www.yacenter.org/young-americans-bank

Do I need more than money to open a savings or checking account?

Yes. You need a Social Security number (SSN). In most states, you are assigned a Social Security number at birth. You also may need a picture ID.

What are some of the online sources that will get me started in the investment world?

- For a tutorial on investing, go to www.investopedia.com/university/beginner/. Another good source is www.stockmarketinvestinginfo.com.

- Many mutual fund investment companies provide online information and training. In order to find the names of mutual fund investment companies, search for "mutual fund companies list." You should come up with lots of choices. A good place to start is with the largest companies based on assets.

- Most news magazines have online services. You can access these sites by searching for the newspaper or magazine name. For example, the Web site of *Kiplinger's Personal Finance* magazine, www.kiplinger.com, gives all sorts of information on investment choices and lets you do calculations on your holdings.

If I don't have access to a computer, how do I find out information on saving and investing?

- The first place to start is the library. Start by looking in the catalog under "investing," "economy," "stocks," "bonds," or "stock market."

- Another good resource is a bookstore that has a business section. You can find a book to answer almost any question you have.

- Check out newspapers and news magazines that are just about business and finance. Resources include the *Wall Street Journal* (daily), *Barron's* (weekly), *Forbes* (weekly), *Kiplinger's Personal Finance* (monthly), *Money* (monthly), and *Smart Money* (monthly).

Are there any resources for investment information specifically geared toward young investors?

- The most exciting way to learn about money, saving, and investing is online. There are dozens of interactive sites where you can play investing games and even set up a virtual portfolio. Many of these sites provide current stock prices when you fill in a stock symbol.

- Check out www.kidsbank.com to learn about money, savings, checking accounts, and investing—with cartoon characters as your guide.

- For money games, go to www.usmint.gov/kids/games.

- For virtual tours of the U.S. Department of the Treasury, go to www.treasury.gov/education. The same site also has links for kids to other parts of the U.S. government. Just follow the links and see what you find. It's all fun. In addition, when you're at the Department of the Treasury site, click on "Bonds and Securities" to learn everything you need to know about U.S. Savings Bonds— where to buy them, what the interest rates are, and how to redeem them.

- There is a NOVA presentation that tells the history of money and how U.S. money is printed and minted at www.pbs.org/wgbh/nova/moolah/. It teaches you a lot, plus it's illustrated with time lines and pictures of money.

- At www.mysavingsquest.com, you can pick a job, set a savings goal, and draw up a budget. This site helps you think in terms of the whole picture: what it's like to budget in order to save.

- You can find free business news at www.bloomberg.com. This is an excellent source because you can find current CD rates, lists of mutual funds, and economic and political news that could affect the market.

How do I find the names of online brokers?

- Go to www.investorguide.com/links-dir-brokerlist.html. The site lists brokers and gives a short description of what they offer and the costs of trades. From the list you can click on any broker's name to go directly to their online site. Some online brokers offer special services like online lessons on investing basics. Fees for trades vary according to the extra services offered, so always check the price. Since you can get free online training from a number of the sites I've listed above, you don't need to pay for anything but the actual trade costs.

- Another way to compare costs and services of electronic brokers is to go to www.fool.com/how-to-invest. This site also provides guidelines for electronic investing.

What does it mean when people talk about a "bull" or a "bear" market?

Bulls and bears are used as symbols for the stock market—a raging bull and a sleeping bear. A *bull market* is one in which investors have confidence in the economy and buy stocks. The stock market goes up over a period of months or years. A *bear market* is one where the market is sluggish and investors are selling stocks and waiting to see what happens. The stock market goes down over a period of months or years. You will also hear investors referred to as "bullish" or "bearish" about the stock market. This means the same thing as above, but it refers to how individuals choose to invest.

Will I be taxed on the money I earn on my savings account and investments?

Yes, if it is over a certain amount. In 2009 that amount was $1,900, but it changes over time. It is best to check the current tax rules at www.irs.gov/taxtopics/tc553.html.

Is there an online source that calculates compound interest?

- A simple site is www.csgnetwork.com/compoundsavingcalc.html.

- Another site that allows you to add to your initial savings each month is www.calculatorweb.com. With this site you can see how much money you will have in the future based on your savings plan.

- You can also use www.bankrate.com/calculators.aspx. It will also calculate car payments and mortgage costs.

Where do I find a list of the different types of mutual funds?

For a description of the various types of mutual funds, go to www.investopedia.com/university/mutualfunds/mutualfunds1.asp.

What are some of the categories of mutual funds that I'll see most often?

- **Balanced:** A fund that is a combination of common and preferred stocks. There's a low risk of loss on the original investment and a pretty good chance for long-term growth. These are classified as a growth-and-income fund.

- **Equity income:** Blue-chip stocks and utilities that pay high dividends. These funds involve limited risk to your original investment with medium long-term growth. These are classified as a growth-and-income fund.

- **Aggressive growth:** Stocks of new companies or companies that fund managers think are selling for less than they are worth. These involve above-average risk. These are classified as a growth fund.

- **Emerging markets:** Stocks in companies in developing countries like Mexico or Russia that involve more risk than other growth fund types. These are classified as a growth fund.

- **Small-cap:** Stocks in new companies that have a limited amount of capital behind them. These have a higher level of risk and are classified as a growth fund.

- **Mid-cap:** Stocks in companies that have a moderate level of capital, have a medium level of risk, and are classified as a growth fund.
- **Large-cap:** Stocks in well-established companies that have a large amount of capital, a lower level of risk, and are classified as a growth-and-income fund.

Are there any basic resource books that could help me get started?

- *The Wall Street Journal Guide to Understanding Money & Investing, Third Edition* by Kenneth M. Morris and Virginia B. Morris (New York: Lightbulb Press, 2004) is a clear and easy-to-use guide to money, stocks, bonds, mutual funds, and the stock market. It also covers the Board of Governors of the Federal Reserve System and the economy. Plus it's small and easy to carry in a backpack.
- *Standard & Poor's Dictionary of Financial Terms* by Virginia B. Morris and Kenneth M. Morris (New York: Lightbulb Press, 2007) is another useful handbook.
- *The 100 Best Stocks You Can Buy 2010* by Peter Sander and John Slatter, CFA (Avon, MA: Adams Media, 2009), is an excellent resource for collecting information on stocks. Although the author includes only 100 stock companies, each company is considered a good buy for an individual investor.

Are there other things to invest in beside stocks, bonds, and mutual funds?

Yes, there are a lot of other things, such as real estate. Remember, Billy Ray invested in land. People also invest in collectibles. *Collectibles* are things that have a value that may increase above what you paid for them, such as baseball cards, old records, or first-edition books that still have their original book jackets. Some people collect Civil War items, arrowheads, or signed baseballs. Other people collect coins, including old coins, newly minted coins, and special edition coins. Some people also buy art made by younger artists with the hope that these artists will become famous later on and their art purchases will increase in value. Almost anything you can think of can be collected; if you choose your collections well, you can enjoy them now and eventually sell them for a profit.

$ Thinking of More Questions

Ask some investment questions of your own. Then go on a search for the answers. When you find it, you'll know you are well on your way to calling yourself a financial analyst and expert investor.

Conclusion

THE WRAP-UP, INCLUDING
A REMINDER OF THE GOAL

THAT'S IT. WE'RE done. If you've gotten to this point and read every word
(or nearly every word), you know a lot about investing—probably more
than most people! All your knowledge adds up to one thing: you are now
fluent in the language of business. You know the words to use and how to
use them. That makes me very proud, and you should be proud too. From
now on you will be able to read or listen to the news and understand what
you are reading or hearing. Plus you will know the consequences the news
has on the investment community—which may eventually include you.

This also means that you might well become a star in various school
organizations. Clubs are always wanting people who can keep the record
of dues and who can account for purchases such as trophies or party

decorations. Since you know how to keep a checkbook and how to manage money, you would be the person for the job. Also, if there is an investing club at your school, I could see you teaching everyone what the best type of investments would be to meet the club's goal.

Now, what happened to Billy Ray since he decided to build equity in his farm? By Thanksgiving 2000, Billy Ray was 23. He graduated from Georgetown College with a double major in business and communications. He was no longer playing basketball, but he's still known as "the Legend" in Mount Sterling. In fact, in March 2001, Billy Ray's name was added to the 10th Region Basketball Hall of Fame. He decided he wanted to get a real estate license so he could help other people buy and sell houses. He studied hard and passed the Kentucky real estate exam. Now he has his license, but that's not his main job.

Billy Ray thought a lot about what he wanted to do after college, and he shopped around for jobs. He decided to take a job as a loan officer at a bank. A loan officer looks at the assets and equity of people who want to take out loans from the bank and then decides if the bank should lend money to them—just like when Billy Ray himself went to the bank for small business loans and a home mortgage.

On February 24, 2001, Billy Ray married his college sweetheart, Micah Robinson. At first they lived in the garage with the bathroom and tiny kitchen. But then they had enough equity in their land to build a house. As you can imagine, Billy Ray hadn't stopped planning. First he bought a piece of investment property, and then he built a duplex, or two attached units, to rent out. He plans to use the rent money to pay the cost of the mortgage loan, and he'll sit back and wait for the value of the property to go up.

A few years ago, Billy Ray switched jobs. He is now the general manager of the Judy Water Association. In 2008 he ran for a seat in the 74th District of Kentucky's House of Representatives. He did not win, but that didn't slow him down. Now, in addition to his full-time job, he is an assistant coach for the Montgomery County High School varsity basketball team, the Indians. That's the same team he led to the Kentucky Boys State Basketball Tournament in 1995 when he was in high school. He's also a father now. He and Micah have two children, Luke and Erin Grace. Go, Billy Ray!

GLOSSARY

APR: Annual or annualized percentage rate.

assets: The value of an individual's or a company's property and possessions.

automated teller machine (ATM): Machines placed in convenient locations that allow you to withdraw money from or deposit money into your checking or savings accounts.

back-end load: The commission paid to the broker or fund family when selling shares in a mutual fund. The fees are stated in percentages of the total dollar amount of the trade.

bank statement: A monthly record from the bank that lists the withdrawals from and deposits made to an account. The end number is the balance of your account on the date the bank mailed the statement.

bond: An agreement between two parties allowing one to borrow money from the other for a set period of time in return for interest.

broker: A person who buys or sells stocks or bonds for individual investors through an exchange. All brokers have to pass a national test in order to trade stocks and bonds.

brokerage house: An investment company that is a member of a stock exchange. The membership allows the brokerage house to trade stocks through the exchange.

capital: The money or other assets that a company uses to start and operate a business.

certificate of deposit (CD): A savings device that pays interest based on a deposit for a specified length of time. The longer the term of the certificate agreement, the higher the interest rate paid.

check register: The section in a checkbook where each check written is recorded.

checking account: Money deposited in a bank and used to make purchases in place of cash. The money in the account is accessed by writing checks, by using your check or debit card, or by doing ATM transactions.

compound interest: One method of accumulating interest over time. Interest is added to the original savings amount at set time periods, such as once a month, and the saver earns interest on the interest paid the previous month. Compounding periods can vary from daily to monthly to quarterly (3 months) to semiannually (6 months).

consumer confidence: Consumers' (or spenders') attitudes about the health of the economy. Confidence determines how freely consumers will spend.

corporate bond: A contract between an investor and a private company. The investor agrees to lend the company money for a set period of time, and in exchange the investor receives interest paid by the company.

credit card: A card that allows you to make a purchase without cash, with the understanding that you will pay at a later date.

debit card: A card that allows you to purchase items with money from your checking account without writing a check. Also called a check card.

dividend reinvestment plan (DRIP): An agreement between an investor and a company that allows the investor to buy more stock with his dividends instead of taking the dividends in cash.

Dow Jones Industrial Average (DJIA), or "the Dow": The daily closing price—shown as an average—of 30 stocks listed on the New York Stock Exchange. The Dow is used as a scorecard for the stock market for the day.

economics: The science of the production and distribution of wealth.

economist: A person who studies and manages the production and distribution of wealth.

economy: The wealth and resources of communities of all sizes, such as towns, cities, states, and nations. The word *economy* comes from a Greek word that means "household management."

equity: The remaining value of a piece of property after subtracting the amount left to pay on the mortgage. You must take into account both the amount of the loan already paid back and the increased or decreased value of the property to get an accurate equity amount.

Federal Reserve System, or "the Fed": The United States' national banking system.

front-end load: The commission paid to the broker or fund family when purchasing shares in a mutual fund. The fees are stated in percentages of the dollar amount of the trade.

inflation: An increase in prices. When prices go up, the value of money goes down because it cannot buy as much.

interest: Money paid for the use of money lent.

invest: To commit money in order to earn a financial return.

limit order: A stock sale or purchase made at a price that is above or below the set price order. A limit order will only be filled if it is to the investor's benefit. The order can be open for a day ("day order") or until the investor cancels it ("good-till-canceled order," or GTC).

line of credit: A set amount of money available to borrow against as needed. Interest is charged only on the amount of money borrowed, not on the total amount of credit available.

macroeconomics: The branch of economics that studies the big picture, such as how many people are working, what they are getting paid, and how many trucks and cars are being produced.

market order: A stock trade made at the current market price. The stock shares are bought or sold as soon as the broker places the order.

microeconomics: The branch of economics that studies individual companies and the consumer response to them.

money market account: A type of savings account purchased through a bank or investment company. Money market accounts offer higher interest rates than straight savings accounts.

mortgage: A contract between a borrower and lender to buy property. The lender is usually a bank or savings and loan company. The borrower pays the lender interest on a monthly basis for the use of the money.

municipal bond: A contract between an investor and a municipality. The investor agrees to lend the municipality money for a set period of time, and in exchange the investor receives interest paid by the municipality.

mutual fund: An investment company that buys groups of stocks or bonds to fit a certain investment goal. Investors are sold shares in the fund.

NASDAQ: National Association of Securities Dealers Automated Quotation.

NYSE: New York Stock Exchange.

portfolio: The stocks and bonds in a mutual fund. *Portfolio* also means the stocks and bonds owned by an investor.

portfolio manager: A person trained to buy and sell stocks or bonds in order to meet the goals of a stock or bond fund.

principal: The original sum of an investment.

recession: A temporary decline in prosperity and economic activity.

return: The profit of an investment.

risk tolerance: The level of risk that a person feels comfortable taking.

savings account: Money kept by a bank or savings-and-loan company. The bank or savings-and-loan company pays you interest to use your money for its lending business.

savings-and-loan company: A privately owned company that offers savings accounts at slightly higher rates of interest than banks. Savings-and-loan companies also lend money.

Securities and Exchange Commission (SEC), or "the Commission": The controlling body in charge of stock and bond markets in the United States. The SEC sets the rules for the stock and bond markets, investigates problems, and sets penalties.

shareholder: A person who owns a share or shares of stock in a company.

simple interest: A percentage of interest paid for a set period of time, such as six months or one year.

stock: The capital of a company.

stock exchange: A company where shares of stock are bought and sold.

stock share: A portion of the capital of a company.

stop order: A stock trade at a set price. The stock shares are bought or sold the moment the market price hits the price set by the investor. The order can be open for a day ("day order") or until the investor cancels it ("good-till-canceled order," or GTC order).

treasury bill, note, and **bond:** A contract between an investor and the U.S. government. The investor agrees to lend the government money for a set period of time, and in exchange the investor receives interest paid by the government.

U.S. Savings Bond: A specific type of contract between an investor and the U.S. government. The government agrees to pay the individual an agreed upon amount of money in exchange for a loan for a set number of years.

yield: The income return on an investment.

Index

ABOUT THE AUTHOR

Katherine Bateman has had diverse interests for as long as she can remember. In her first career, she was an art historian and a college professor. She received her BA from Berea College in Berea, Kentucky, and her MA and PhD from the University of Michigan in Ann Arbor. She also completed postdoctoral work at the University of Chicago. Bateman taught art history at Berea College and the School of the Art Institute of Chicago. During this career, she published articles and presented research papers on early medieval manuscripts and ivories. After thirteen years of teaching, she decided to start over.

Her second career was in business. In 1983 she joined Nuveen Investments and began to teach herself the language of business. During this career, she published handbooks to guide brokers and their clients on various topics, including savings programs for college educations and retirement. She also served as the financial advisor for the Illinois Educational Facilities Authority, through which private colleges and universities could access the bond market in order to build dormitories, stadiums, and other facilities. Bateman was active in the National Federation of Municipal Analysts (NFMA), which represents institutional investors. In her role as an officer with the NFMA, she worked closely with the U.S. Securities and Exchange Commission to develop industry guidelines for the municipal market; Bateman testified before Congress regarding the regulation of municipal bonds. The *Bond Buyer*, *Institutional Investor*, and *Smith's Research & Ratings Review* named her the leading analyst in higher education.

In the spring of 2000, Bateman retired from Nuveen Investments to write books—a desire she has had since childhood. In addition to the first and second editions of *The Young Investor*, Bateman published *Kentucky Clay: Eleven Generations of a Southern Dynasty* in November 2008. She lives in Oak Park, Illinois.